Who then are the true philosophers?
Those, I said, who are lovers of the vision of truth,
...they are lovers of all true being.

Plato

Occidental logic is the logic that takes things as its
object, while Oriental logic is the logic that takes
mind as its object . . . in the logic of Buddhism, I
think, there are the germs of a logic that takes the self
as its object — — a logic of the mind.

Kitarō Nishida

SUNY Series in Buddhist Studies
Kenneth K. Inada, Editor

The Logic Of Unity

The Discovery of Zero and Emptiness in Prajñāpāramitā *Thought*

HŌSAKU MATSUO

Translated by

KENNETH K. INADA

State University of New York Press

Ichi-no-ronri (The Logic of Unity)
Originally published in Japanese
by
Hokuju Shuppan Co., Ltd.
Tokyo, 1981

Published by
State University of New York Press, Albany

©1987   State University of New York

For information, address State University of New York
Press, State University Plaza, Albany, N.Y., 12246

Library of Congress Cataloging-in-Publication Data

Matsuo, Hōsaku, 1901–85
The logic of unity.

   (SUNY series in Buddhist studies)
   Translation of: Ichi-no-ronri.
   Includes index.
   1. Philosophy, Buddhist   2. Philosophy, Comparative.
3. Knowledge, theory of (Buddhism)   I. Title.
II. Series.
B162.M3713   1987   121   86-5916
ISBN 0-88706-391-8
ISBN 0-88706-392-6 (pbk.)

10 9 8 7 6 5 4 3 2 1

Contents

Chapter II   The Logic of Unity   *57*

    — Discovery of zero and emptiness in prajñāpāramitā *thought —*

Chapter III   The Truth in the *Heart Sūtra*   *103*

Foreword

In the development of social action, an idea is required for its foundation. To assert, however mildly, that an idea is unnecessary is, afterall, an idea. And since man thinks, wills, and acts, it is impossible that he lives without any ideas.

Now, since the end of the war in 1945 and to the present, a crucial question can be posed: "Has the Japanese world of thought fully met the challenge and demands of the times?" Or, is it not the case that various ideas have merely been tossed about without any real focus?

I wish to call your attention to Dr. Hōsaku Matsuo, who has given deep thought to the matter. Highly respected by people in diverse fields of endeavor, he is a most distinguished physician in the city of Kanazawa, Ishikawa Prefecture. Immediately after the war, he led an ideological movement of scholars to gain new directions and has admirably maintained its activities through the years. As a starting point, he candidly asserts: "Philosophy is the very foundation of man's education and should not be relegated to an ineffective discipline as it exists today." (p. 48)

What then would be the best course of action? Since there are many philosophical ideas in the world, each asserting its own perspective and meaning of existence, a resolution must be found based on self-evidence and mutual examination of all ideas. Dr. Matsuo expands: "Here there is a need for comparative thought as a learning process, one established by mutual agreement in the academic world, in short, a truly comparative philosophy. It must have a generalizing effect involving both public opinion and the learning process." (pp. 3–4)

He has long been a staunch advocate of comparative thought and comparative philosophy. Although academic circles in the past did not pay much attention to his pleas for comparative ideological studies, in recent years, scholars, as well as the general public, have begun to listen.

His long engagement in comparative pursuits has resulted in the present work, *The Logic of Unity*. The exposition covers many areas, and, though it would be extremely difficult to achieve unanimity of opinion from specialists of diverse fields, the work itself is extremely valuable for its sincere and bold analysis. Granted that research by specialists must be respected at all times. Still, when it comes to questions on man's existence, the desideratum is to start afresh by avoiding any preconceived notions. From this point of view, then, Dr. Matsuo has valiantly confronted the basic problems of life and society. This is an important step in promoting new directions and accommodation in the face of conflicts as we look to the future.

I highly value and recommend this work for its total detachment of preconceptions and its bold ideological unfoldment.

Hajime Nakamura

Emeritus Professor, University of Tokyo
President, Japanese Association of Comparative Philosophy

Translator's Introduction

I first met Dr. Hōsaku Matsuo in the autumn of 1975 in Tokyo, in conjunction with a meeting of the Japanese Association of Comparative Philosophy. A few weeks later, through the good offices of Dr. Hajime Nakamura, I was invited to visit Dr. Matsuo at his home in the city of Kanazawa. He escorted me by taxi to the historic sites in and out of the city, such as, the most beautiful Kenroku-en (Park) and the famous Kanazawa Castle which now houses the main campus of the University of Kanazawa, including visits to the old haunts and memorial places of two of Kanazawa's most influential intellectual giants—Kitarō Nishida and Daisetz T. Suzuki.

We stayed together over a weekend at a lovely quiet Japanese inn, ensconced in the deep valleys outside of the city, and discussed quite casually the many aspects and problems of comparative philosophy in general and Buddhist thought in particular. In the course of the conversations, I began to feel a definite affinity with his philosophical views and to admire his unbounded enthusiasm for comparative work. I also began to respect him as a physician and discovered to my delight that his avocation in philosophy was not only genuine but funded with more than ordinary knowledge. This gentle man had, indeed, a most penetrative mind rarely encountered in any circle. His depth and breadth of philosophical knowledge, both East and West, was simply astounding, in light of the fact that philosophy was not his special field nor was he trained in it. In Western tradition, he immediately reminded me of the British empiricist, John Locke, who likewise was trained as a physician and who eventually left a huge mark in Western epistemology.

In 1981, he published *The Logic of Unity (Ichi-no-ronri)*, the fruition of his long years of deliberation on the problems of methodology. He sent me a copy, and I examined it carefully. I wrote him back immediately to say that the work was indeed a singular contribution to the field of comparative thought, and it ought to have a wider audience beyond Japanese shores. The idea of an English translation was spawned. He approached me on the matter. I, of course, agreed to do it but not immediately, as I had other commitments which kept me occupied for the better half of 1983.

It was a pleasure to meet Dr. Matsuo again in Tokyo in November of 1982 and to discuss the details of the translation project. He gave me then full authority and freedom to translate the work in the best manner possible to faithfully convey its main ideas. I have subsequently added more notes for clarification and expansion and a glossary of terms for the serious reader. I must also note that I have deleted from the translation Chapter IV on Twenty-five Questions and Answers (pp. 179–201 of the Japanese text) and the Appendix on What is Democracy? (pp. 202–235) due to the repetitive nature of the discussion, much of which is already embodied in the previous sections, and the specific treatment of democratic principles that are only applicable and relevant to Japanese society. It should be noted that the discussion of the postwar Japanese Constitution and its reference and meaning to the people and state are interpreted within the context of his methodology and are both provocative and illuminating.

The careful reader will undoubtedly sense the close affinity and accord of the present work with those of the members of the Kyoto School[1] of philosophy and religion, founded and based on the writings of Kitarō Nishida. As mentioned earlier, Nishida was a native son of Kanazawa and is considered today to be the foremost seminal philosopher of modern Japan. Although not a direct disciple, Matsuo had read and greatly benefitted from the writings of Nishida and, indeed, has carried on the philosophical tradition as if he were an essential part of that tradition. Though the ideological lineage is quite apparent, it would not do to push the matter too far in any narrow sense. Matsuo is an independent thinker with a different professional background but still belonging to the intellectual and cultural complex of Japan which is steeped in Buddhist thought and action. The source from which Nishida philosophy springs is a common ground and spirit of the Japanese; thus, to be overly critical of a certain school of thought by selective analysis, comparison, and accommodation would tend to foster merely simple and abstract understanding and may eventually end in superficial treatment of the profound ideas that are present and constantly intersecting in the total philosophical posture of the Japanese.

Nishida's self-acclaimed system of 'self-consciousness of absolute nothingness' with its attendant unique doctrines of 'the self-identity of absolute contradiction' and 'the logic of place' present a truly novel philosophy of the present. At the same time, from the very outset, it has two important facets that mark it off as a most viable system: on the one hand, it brings forth the challenge to probe, refine, and develop further into the context of the present moment as the locus of reality, and, on the other, it impels one to search deeper into the roots of the ideological basis in the cultural complex, especially in the Buddhist tradition. To this extent, Nishida philosophy is an open-ended system. Indeed, it is to his credit that after the maiden work, *The Study of Good (Zen-no-kenkyū)*,[2] he wholeheartedly engaged himself in the probe for the basis of ultimate reality in 'pure experience' (*junsui-keiken*) with all the force of intutition, dialectic, and logic at his command by exposing himself sensitively to both Eastern and Western thought. About fifteen years later he had succeeded in that probe with his capping work, *From the Acting to the Seeing (Hataraku-mono-kara-miru-mono-e)*, published in 1927. Since then, the open-ended texture of 'pure experience' has resulted in original works in different facets by his direct and indirect disciples up to the very present. And perhaps it was not a mere coincidence that Nishida formulated the concept of 'pure experience', having been influenced by William James' works, for one of the fundamental features of both Nishida and James is admission of the multifaceted nature of experience itself or what James himself preferred to label, 'radical empiricism'. Pragmatism is a recurriung theme in Western philosophy, never dominant or taking the lead in any movement — academically, socially, or politically. Yet is it most prominent in all discussions, from logic to religious matters, for it has offered us one of the most stable and reliable forms of truth, the pragmatic theory of truth, which we overtly or covertly entertain in our everyday lives.

Nishida's thought did not move along pragmatic lines but explored deeper into the noetic basis of man. His great contribution lies in the fresh and vigorous approach to epistemology grounded in Oriental thought but flexible and open enough to accommodate Western religious and philosophical elements. In brief, his system maintained a truly universal character for creative thrusts in many directions; indeed, his final essays reveal the intercultural, international dimensions of his system.[3] Matsuo naturally has taken up the challenge in his own way but with a particular eye on the establishment of a methodology that has universal and experiential appeal and cogency. He is still a child of his own culture, as Nishida and others are, in keeping a good focus on the momentary present within the organic whole as the foundation of a dynamic epistemology. Just as the case was with Nishida, Matsuo, too, is enthralled by the function and strength of logic and mathematics, the backbones of the sciences, to give determination to certain aspects of the momentary present; indeed, he sees the sciences extending properly into the social and humanistic areas and that our experiences, being basically dialectical in nature, can be brought before the tribunal of 'dialectical logic' for a singular unifying vision of things. Thus he has aptly entitled his work *The Logic of Unity*.

Incidentally, D. T. Suzuki has mentioned that Nishida became intensely interested in Kegon (Hua-yen) thought rather late in life.[4] This may be so, but, in many respects, his knowledge of and familiarity with Zen had already implicated Kegon thought into his system, since Zen is infused with it.[5] But, where Nishida had incorporated Kegon thought later or implicitly, Matsuo does it from the very beginning, including doctrines from other works such as the *Heart Sūtra* and *Awakening of Faith in the Mahāyāna*.

The Logic of Unity is a bold attempt to bring to focus a new perspective in epistemology, an inquiry into the very foundations of man in a truly holistic sense. Not only is the nature of man under scrutiny but also the profoundly dynamic way in which he is seen within the total nature of things. In doing so, the quintessential doctrine of emptiness (*śūnyatā*), especially as expounded in the *Heart Sūtra*, is invoked to exhibit the unique way in which the so-called 'realization or consciousness of the mind-base' manifests and functions. This is a revolutionary conception but one that is so close to each of us, i.e., potentially present and activated in all epistemological activities. The understanding of this function is, according to Matsuo's analysis, the very foundation of epistemology and indeed the important link in any dialogue. The details still require working out, and he is the first to admit its preliminary nature. In this respect, the work is unfinished. Yet he has tendered to us a most profound and rare challenge in comparative analysis that goes deeply into every area of human endeavor. For him, the understanding of the distinct rise of the nature of 'intuitive unconscious' is the point of departure in any methodology, in any comparative social and scientific thought, and ultimately in all East-West dialogues. He has undoubtedly ventured far into the very basic frontier of epistemic function and has brought into play the central experiential elements of Buddhist thought within the context of conventional epistemological characteristics of man. In this respect, he has presented us with a novel prolegomenon to comparative methodology and philosophy, albeit a crystallization and application of centuries old Buddhist thought boldly framed within the realm of truth sought by man and society in this turbulent world. Not only does it bind the various disciplines together, but it also allows them to consult with each other and to move ahead into future discourses with courage, confidence, and harmony. I hope, to some measure at least, I have succeeded in bringing forth the sense and spirit of his philosophical insights.

Since the work was written originally for the Japanese audience, the author is quite critical of the Japanese postwar mentality and attitudes. In a later section which is not translated here, he sings high praise of the new Japanese Constitution and saw it as a golden opportunity to realize the truly democratic principles in the Japanese way of life, a return to the historical and momentous period ushered in by Prince Shōtoku (573–621) with the promulgation of the Mahāyāna Buddhist ideal. Here however he has touched on the Constitution and the Basic Education Law in a peripheral way. The tone of his writing is patronizing to a degree, but it is always supported by traditional Buddhist, Shintō, and Confucian principles.

For the non-Japanese reader, the paucity of references to the various Western philosophies and philosophers, especially those in the twentieth century, may cause some annoyance, uneasiness, and even puzzlement, but traditional Japanese writings are usually characterized by focus on the essential problems or issues at hand, even at the expense of glossing over men and systems. If references are made, they are customarily concise and abbreviated. There is much assumed on the part of both reader and writer, and some ideas are expressed in terse, aphoristic style. This work is no exception; thus, the references throughout the work are kept to a minimum. The important point, nevertheless, is that his contributions stand alone and can be seen in a clear light despite the lack of references to men and philosophies of the modern period.

Western philosophers as a rule have difficulty accommodating Eastern thought, not for lack of curiosity or interest but because there is a built-in bias against an alien thought which cannot be funnelled through their self-imposed empirical, analytic, and linguistic mills. The present work may be a prime candidate of that bias. However, as the author makes it abundantly clear, philosophy of whatever persuasion must return to the basics, to the holistic nature of man, and with renewed vigor and enthusiasm reminiscent of Grecian times begin to raise the fundamental question, "What is man?" and delve deeper into the pre-bias nature of things.

It remains finally for me to acknowledge those who have been vital in the progress of the translation. Foremost, of course, is Dr. Hajime Nakamura for his initial suggestion, contact, and continued interest and advice on all phases of the project. To Dr. Hideo Mineshima for his warm personal encouragement even after the untimely and sudden death of the author in September 1985. To Nolan P. Jacobson for reading through an earlier draft of the manuscript and providing me with some helpful suggestions for improvement. And to Michele Martin of SUNY Press for her sustained interest in the manuscript and for seeing through the onerous job of its publication. To all, I express my heartfelt gratitude and appreciation. Whatever errors or shortcomings that exist are strictly mine.

Kenneth K. Inada

State University of New York at Buffalo

Preface

Why Philosophy?

In this small work, I would like to touch upon some of the reasons for the need of philosophy and comparative philosophy.

In regard to the first, the need of philosophy, it was Karl Jaspers who said that we are presently in the second 'axial age'. The first axial age, of course, refers to the period approximatley 500 B.C., spread two or three hundred years in either direction, in which the world had seen, in succession, the appearance of famous philosophic giants, such as, Socrates, Plato, and Aristotle in the West and the Buddha, Confucius, and Lao Tzu in the East. It can be speculated that the age bespeaks of the dramatic transformation in civilization on the one hand and the great confused ideological state of affairs on the other. Presumably, the appearance of a great thinker does not happen at random in a society which has no need of one. But, assuming that such a thinker were to appear in an indifferent society, there would certainly be no following and no sustained remembrance and respect for one throughout the ages.

At any rate, we are possibly in the second axial age. Since the seventeenth and eighteenth centuries, the tremendous advances made in the natural sciences have created a world that is becoming increasingly small, a world where various peoples can communicate with each other in a monolithic sense. On the other hand, since ideology and religion did not keep pace with the scientific advances, the thought process of peoples of the world remained uneven and divided and a fortiori in great confusion. Although we have witnessed horrendous cruelties and brutalities committed by and on man in both the First and Second World Wars, there is no indication that the ideological confusion has abated, and, in the current situation, there is a distinct possibility of a third world war. It goes without saying that the next war would be so devastating that the survival of the human race would be in jeopardy.

In truth, it would seem that the current economic and political conditions are reminiscent of a child playing with firecrackers in a burning house, casually going about serving its own needs and pleasures—all of which makes us yearn all the more for the appearance of an appropriate great thinker.

After the war in Japan, the Education Rescript, which had heretofore formed the pillar of the educational process, was abolished and replaced by a democracy heralded immediately as the greatest principle of life. When the citizens are questioned on the true nature of democracy, however, there is hardly any philosophical understanding of it, and, in truth, it exists without digestion, merely as a formal conception. For, does the mere increase in the number of colleges and universities create a cultured nation? Does the mere relinquishment of arms create a peaceful nation? A rude awakening certainly awaits all, if the distinction between ordinary thought process and the discipline of true philosophic function is not made clearly. It is imperative that philosophy becomes a unique science, a functional reality, and, if you will, that it addresses directly the question on the nature of man qua man. Moreover, the question may be extended to the nature of the mind, that is, to an inquiry into how the mind really functions. This is not merely a psychological study of the mind so current today. Rather than what is done in ordinary psychology, it must be one that probes the very foundations of man's mental activity.

The impression one gets of the present status of philosophy is that it is far from being a viable discipline. It was known in the past as the queen of the sciences, the first science or the most essential science of learning. This was when it was still conceived of as a science of the mind, i.e., a humanistic science. Yet, in the case of Japan, no sooner had democracy arrived than the troubles began with strife in the universities and with riots and suicides even down in middle and high schools. Do such troubles describe the presence of a viable philosophy of a cultured nation? The fundamentals of education do not lie in following the leading edges of technology and technics but rather in the implementation of so-called human education or education of the mind, focusing on the real need for a viable philosophy of life.

Why Comparative Philosophy?

Philosophy is the pursuit of many diverse ways of thinking, man's ideas, and, in this sense, it is the science of ideas. To be sure, man's way of thinking will differ in accordance with differences based on history, environmental conditions, and cultural tradition. My personal view, however, is that there is but one truth in the world. Although a view is an expression of truth asserted by respective individuals, nevertheless, if there are as many assertions and truths derived as there are individuals, then any assertion or any view would be taken to be the truth and man could go on to do anything he pleases to justify himself. In such a chaotic situation, any ideologue could claim the truth of his own assertion while, at the same time, deny the presence of other truths. Moreover, in the present condition of ideological freedom and the attendant mutually clashing views, there would inevitably arise a state of ideational confusion in the absence of a true philosophy as a science of inquiry.

Despite this expressed call for a true philosophy in this allegedly second axial age, I do not believe that this is an age in which the appearance of a great philosopher would be able to command the attention of the people to reflect on their shortcomings as they did in the past. In the present age, though the number could not be very high, nevertheless, there would be at least one or two great philosophers. The world is, after all, so wide and open. Yet, in spite of the presence of a great philosopher, the failure to command the same persuasive and propagative power of still another Buddha or Jesus must be attributed to the conditions of our times. Here then is a definite need for comparative thought as a learning process, one established by mutual agreement in the academic world, in short, a truly comparative philosophy. It must have a generalizing effect, involving both public opinion and learning process. However, in order to realize a comparative philosophy based on various ideological views, there must be a methodology of comparative philosophy that is agreeable to all. This would mean that the methodology would be based on the dictum, "know thyself," the words of Socrates, and "make unto yourself the light; make the Dharma your light," the words of the Buddha. Regardless of geographic and periodic separation, it is clearly seen that there is a remarkable similarlity in the foundation of East and West philosophies which presages the possibility of a single methodology and comparative philosophy.

The fundamental meeting point in East-West philosophy is in the simple dictum: "Truth is in thyself." Up to now, however, for the most part we have been seeking the truth in some distant external realm, whereas in reality it has always been so close to us. A famous Chinese poem says, in effect, that one may set out in search of spring all day long but may not be successful. One may roam all over, but it may still elude him like a vanishing cloud. As one trods homeward, passing under the plum blossom, spring is in full array at the tip of the branches!

When the Dharma (i.e., Buddhist truth of existence) is spoken of, it simply refers to the fact that there is a structure at its basis. Similarly, the discovery of the heliocentric theory by Copernicus means that he had discovered the relationship of appearance and reality in the structure of the universe. The same can be said of Newton's discovery of the principles of universal gravitation. So long as the structure of the universe does not change, the principles of universal gravitation may be correlated as the truth of existence, the unchanging truth of the universe, and the appearance or nonappearance of Newton has nothing to do with the truth.

Philosophic truth is similar in nature to physical truth. In general Western thought, heretofore the search for the truth was keyed to something external to the self or within the Logos. But I believe the search is really of the mind itself, i.e., seeking for the unchanging principles inherent to the structure of the thinking or cognitive process. The function of true philosophy is then to know thyself in terms of understanding the structure of one's own thinking process. Perceived in this way, the meaning of the Buddhist assertion, "The Dharma is unchanging regardless of the appearance or nonappearance of the Buddha," would become clear and so would the assertion that the truth is unchanging in the East and West.

The so-called structure of man's thinking is not easily known or understood, in spite of the advances made in medical science or cerebral physiology. Put another way, the structure of the mind with which one philosophizes is the same structure with which one does geometry or ordinary mathematics. No separate minds are required to engage in philosophy and the natural sciences. If the truth derived is the same truth regardless of whether it is a Westerner or an Easterner doing mathematics or natural sciences, the respective answers being essentially the one and only truth, then why is a diversity of truths entertained only in philosophy? This cannot be the case. In the pursuit of the uniqueness of truth lies the key to a methodology in comparative philosophy.

Last June, I edited a book, *Hikaku-tetsugaku-hōhōron-no-kenkyū (Studies in the Methodology of Comparative Philosophy)*,[1] which was the result of three years of intense dialogues among select members of the Japanese Association for Comparative Thought and focussed on methodological studies. As the work was mainly addressed to scholars, having many difficult passages, it did not attract the attention of the general public. But now, in this age of ideational confusion, the language of philosophy and ideology aside, every effort should be made to raise the level of consciousness of all to Immanuel Kant's allusion to "the man who truly philosophizes" or to the dictum, "the man who truly knows himself." Since a philosophy burdened by cant or limited to specialists has no real social force, I decided to write a relatively easy-to-understand treatise on methodology, so that the average person may become aware of and understand such basic questions as "What is man?" or "What is reality?" in the hope of assuring the establishment of true education of man, social consciousness, and democratic principles. I have thus avoided mere linguistic analysis and interpretation as usually found in philosophical writings and have, instead, incorporated examples from ordinary experience, diagrams from mathematics and geometry, and structural sketches of the cognitive process, all of which aid the understanding that truth is really one and that all can be reduced to the dictum: "Know thyself."

It should be noted, however, that this method of inquiry into truth only indicates the direction in which truth is being pursued and that it by no means claims that the provisional diagrams or sketches depict truth itself or that the methodology is unalterable. The value of the methodology could only be determined in terms of the cooperative effort of many minds in treating the numerous issues of the past and present within the various philosophical systems in order to arrive at a unique principle; thus, it would have to await the results of future endeavors. I in no way regard my methodology to be absolute or definitive but rather as a point of departure in the whole enterprise. Speaking from another aspect, I am quite mindful of the fact that as the methodology is revised there will certainly be a comparable advance in philosophy itself. Consequently, I would never for a minute think of avoiding any dialogue and suggestions for improvements.

Western and Eastern Philosophy

Western philosophy starts with the basic question, "What is it that exists?" In the history of philosophy, this question underlies the basis for everything that exists and was raised initially in search of that 'primal stuff' which is the source of all beings. Parenthetically, in the background of general Western philosophy, without raising the question of approval or disapproval, its basis seems to be pervaded by the Judeo-Christian concept of God.

Many answers havé been offered in response to the basic question over the past several millenia, and these have respectively formed a variety of world views. They have been labelled, for example, as materialism, spiritualism, and hylozoism.[2] When the history of Western philosophy is compared to Buddhist thought, it is interesting to note that the central focus of the latter is not on matter, spirit, or any form of 'nonbeing' (Chinese *wu*; Japanese *mu*) or 'emptiness' (Chinese *k'ung*; Japanese *kū*). In Buddhist thought, moreover, the question of the self is always addressed from its own basis or primal origins. By contrast, speaking on world views in the context of Western tradition, Karl Jaspers made the following observation:[3]

But which is the correct view? Through thousands of years the warring schools have been unable to demonstrate the truth of any one of them . . . Why is this so? All these views have one thing in common: they apprehend being as something which confronts me as an object, which stands apart from me as I think it. This basic phenomenon of our consciousness is to us so self-evident that we barely suspect the riddle it presents, because we do not inquire into it. The thing that we think, of which we speak, is always something other than ourselves, it is the object toward which we as subject are oriented. If we make ourselves into the object of our thinking, we ourselves become as it were the Other, and yet at the same time we remain a thinking I, which thinks about itself but cannot aptly be thought as an object because it determines the objectness of all objects. We call this basic condition of our thinking the subject-object dichotomy. As long as we are awake and conscious we are always involved in it . . . What is the meaning of this ever-present subject-object dichotomy? It can only mean that being as a whole is neither subject nor object but must be the Comprehensive, which is manifested in this dichotomy.

In this way, Jaspers tried to explore the realm beyond the subject-object dichotomy and arrived at the novel idea of the Comprehensive (*das Umgreifende*).

Contemporary Western philosophy, especially existentialism, has come quite close to Eastern views on the philosophy of human nature, in the function of epistemology. But, as Jaspers indicates, past Western philosophy had been concerned mainly with questions on the nature of being which inevitably caused the subject-object dichotomy to arise and thereby precluded the possibility of affirming a singluar reality. In other words, the realization of 'emptiness' was lacking, and the situation remained similar to the period prior to the discovery of the 'zero' in mathematics. From this point of view, Jaspers' discovery of the Comprehensive must be considered a great advancement, but it fell short of the Eastern concept of 'emptiness' as it still carried the notion of an ontological being and could not rise above the currents of Western thought.

Buddhist philosophy expounds cryptically as follows:[4]

Form is not differentiated from emptiness and emptiness is
  not differentiated from form. Form is at once
  emptiness and emptiness is at once form.
Consciousness is not differentiated from emptiness and
  emptiness is not differentiated from consciousness.

Consciousness is at once emptiness and emptiness is at once consciousness.

Not only does the above consummate an epistemology, but it clearly dissolves the subject-object dichotomy. The reason for this is that, where in Western philosophy, as Jaspers says, the subject is an internal condition and the object external, in Buddhist thought the mind as the subject of cognition is likened to the sound of a clear bell or the reception of a television set in which both the subjective and objective components are included in a 'single mind' and the unifying element is the 'zero' concept or the concept of '*prajñā*-emptiness',[5] which does not permit any impediments. This is a special feature of the Buddhist way of thinking which has continued from the original teachings of the Buddha recorded in early Buddhist texts to the Mahāyāna tradition. The feature is amply evidenced in the principles of mathematics, geometry, and in the television set. So, when Buddhism refers to such concepts as the 'mind' or 'consciousness-only', it would be a grave mistake to compare them in terms of Western philosophical correlates, such as, idealism or mentalism.

So now, if a question were to be raised, "What is Eastern philosophy?" the proper reply would be, "It is but a name for the mind." If it were further asked, "What is the mind?" the answer would most certainly be, "It is the substance of philosophy itself." In the following Zen saying,[6] "Directly point at one's mind; perceive its very nature and become the Buddha" (i.e., be enlightened), the aim is to have direct access to one's own essential nature (i.e., realize the mind-source or be conscious of the mind-base) in order to accomplish life's ultimate fulfillment by its clear consciousness. Consequently, philosophy is the resolution of the ultimate questions relating to life which has direct reference to man's fundamental nature of the mind. Being so, it must not deal with abstract matters as treated in philosophy today and known only to philosophers, but, instead, it must be an indispensable discipline open to everyone for the fulfillment of one's own personhood.

Chapter I

Methodology of Comparative Philosophy

—Realization of mind-base and intuitive unconsciousness—

Locus of the Problem and Its Development

Definition and method

The question "What is Philosophy?" seems simple enough, but to the philosopher it is a most difficult one to answer. The matter is aggravated in Western philosophy, since no philosophical question can be treated in any universal sense. The reason for this is that philosophy itself is not a unified discipline but is seen from a variety of viewpoints. For example, some think of it as a form of materialism, some as involved in mere epistemology, and in the twentieth century, as movement in pragmatism, existentialism, and analytic philosophy. It may also be viewed from the perspective of philosophy of religion, philosophy of culture, and philosophy of economics, all attesting to the fact that there are many ways in which philosophy is defined and making it extremely difficult to arrive at a singular meaning.

In Oriental philosophy, especially in Buddhism, the situation is different. With Buddhism, it is said that those who perceive the nature of the true self perceive the Dharma, and those who perceive the Dharma perceive the Buddha (i.e., achieve enlightenment). Zen actively promotes the goal: "Directly point at the mind; perceive the nature of things and become the Buddha." This is the

9

unique way to have intimations of the true nature of the mind, to realize its nature and thereby achieve the aim of life's finality.

The *Kanmuryōjukyō (Amitayur-dhyāna-sūtra: The Sūtra of the Meditation on Amitayus)*, a sutra of the Pure Land School, emphatically states thus:[1]

> The Buddhas and Tathāgatas are the embodiment of *dharmadhātu* (the realm of the *dharmas*, i.e., reality as such). They always enter into the minds and thoughts of all sentient creatures. In consequence, when you are mindful of the Buddha, the mind is at once the manifestation of his thirty-two auspicious major physical features and eighty minor features. The mind creates the Buddha; indeed the mind is the Buddha.

From an early period, Zen has utlized the above thought as seen in the succinct assertion: "This mind is the Buddha; the mind at once is the Buddha." It confirms the fact that the thought is consistent in both the Pure Land and Zen traditions, thus rendering clear and distinct the question, "What is Buddhism?"

Contemporary Western philosophy, by contrast, does not have a clear-cut definition. I, personally, think that this situation in the West bespeaks of the crisis in contemporary European philosophy, i.e., a crisis of ideological confusion. And yet, ironically, when European thought is traced back ultimately to Greek thought, there very much in evidence is the fundamental Socratic viewpoint: "Know thyself." If man's consciousness were not existent, then materialism and ontology would force upon man an alien form of religion and philosophy. Should that be the case, religion and philosophy would be completely irrelevant and meaningless for all. But philosophy is inevitably the study of ideas, and its substance must invariably be a return to the problematics of the mind as focussed so well in Cartesian dictum: "I think, therefore I exist." This is then a problem of the mind, the study of the mind, and everything must lead on to the question, "What is man?" To illustrate by analogies, when one thinks about farming, the method will be described in terms of spades and hoes, and, when the question, "What is fishing?" is raised, its method necessarily will be defined in terms of fishing nets and boats. In this way, the aim and method are directly linked to each other.

My methodology

If philosophy delves in the realm of studying ideas and knowing oneself, then it would have to be in the sense of knowing the very nature of one's mind or knowing the very principles of epistemic function. To say that there is in general a 'principle' means that there is always at its basis a 'structure'. Wouldn't it be fascinating to express this in a geometric sketch? Such a projection will constitute my own meaning of methodology as well as a humble contribution to comparative thought.

On philosophizing

Immanuel Kant's famous words are that the function of philosophy is not to study philosophy itself but to engage in philosophizing. Following these words, I have applied the dictum, "Know thyself." Actually, I am not the first to consider the application of geometry to philosophy in modern times, for it was done earlier by both Spinoza and Descartes. It can be said, however, that in comparison to the brilliant developments in the natural sciences, philosophy did not exhibit comparable developments, a fact which has caused not a few philosophers of the modern age to model their own systems after the sciences. The logic in geometry, however, is still tied to the nature of formal logic in Western philosophy, and, since it establishes itself only when schematized or diagrammed, it is not necessarily possible to demonstrate what philosophy is in terms of a structure of the mind. Kant and Karl Jaspers have said that in Western philosophy there is a lack of synthetic judgment. Ever since Kant, the possibility of synthetic judgment has been an eminent and important subject but without any drastic development, so far. For my part, I have proceeded to schematize and diagram what I consider to be the thinking order of the human intellect based on Oriental thought. These are the diagrams on 'realization or consciousness of mind-base' and 'intuitive unconsciousness'.

I have also examined these diagrams in correspondence with the logic implied in mathematics or in natural numbers. All this will be discussed henceforth under the convenient rubric of "the logic of unity," which is based on my initial lectures presented at Kanazawa University, Japan. Though labelled as lectures, they always involved open discussions with the special students enrolled. The reason that I considered the logic in mathematics or in natural numbers is that in them there is the discovery of the concept of 'zero'. For example, without any schematization and solely relying on natural numbers, it is possible to express the truth as a kind of logic, and thus, by analogy, the changes in the equation will indicate truthfully the function of the human intellect. The 'zero' plays a powerful role in this respect.

The concept of truth can be expressed in an extremely simple and formal manner thus: "What exists is and what does not does not." This does not, however, mean that what is seen exists and what is not seen does not exist. For, indeed, we must take into consideration the fact that what is not seen is also germane to the structure of the mind. Here, there are questions to be posed. For example, is there or is there not such a thing called 'the structure of the mind'? Is there or is there not such an entity called a 'mind'? And what of the existence of the concept of zero in mathematics or the Buddhist concept of emptiness (śūnyatā)? Confronted with these questions, the problem of the nature of cognition inevitably arises.

The logic in natural mathematics (i.e., four principles of arithmetic: addition, subtraction, multiplication, and division) is frequently seen in Buddhist philosophy as, for example, in the 'emptiness of wisdom' of the *Prajñāpāramitā Sūtras* and the "expressible nature of true thusness (*tathatā*): mutual penetration of the one and the many or of being and nonbeing" of the *Treatise on the Awakening of Faith in the Mahāyana*. Although the so-called dialectical logic of the East and the formal logic of the West are based on the same logic found in mathematics, still there is a difference between the logic in natural mathematics, including algebra, and the logic in geometry. The difference demonstrates the reason why Western philosophy cannot accommodate the function of a synthetic judgment. And therein lies the basic difference between Western formal logic and Eastern 'dialectical logic'. That Western philosophy employs a geometric type of logic means that the nature of truth relies solely on the notion of existence based on things seen and that it is determined decisively by the categories of existence and nonexistence, attesting to the fact that a non-diagrammatic geometry solves nothing. If, on the other hand, it were possible to express, not in language but with geometric diagrams, the so-called diagram of the mind-base, then it would be possible to express the heretofore unseen structure of the mind. If that were possible at all, then in that respect there would be a unified basis for thinking in East-West philosophy.

The structure of cognition will differ in accordance with whether it is interpreted in naive, realistic terms or in terms of the receiver of a TV set or the mirror reflection of an image. When we normally view, for example, the Silk Road on the TV set, the road seems to be realistically in the set. But, in actuality, the TV set must first receive the images in order to project them at any time and as many times as programmed. This illustrates the difference between naive realism and the function of epistemology in philosophy, and, though it points up the difference in views, it also means that the realms of realism and epistemology necessarily penetrate each other such that the realm of realism cannot have an independent status. There simply cannot be a confrontation or opposition between the two. Put another way, although we tend to take the truth of things by relying on their existence, there is still the problem of involving man's cognition, a science of man which focuses on his mind, including the sense faculties, and concerns the 'realization or consciousness of the mind-base'. In this day of advancement in the natural sciences, it is only proper that the truth is focussed in the cognitive realm, based on what exists and what does not, and that the search for that truth lies within the domain of philosophy. The 'realization or consciousness of the mind-base' is then the answer to the question "What is man?" and the means of knowing thyself, as well.

I have thus engaged in philosophizing by thinking things through by not being caught up in translated terms or on the printed word in order to arrive at the realization of the mind-base. This is a proposal of a methodology in comparative philosophy, as well as my definition of philosophy itself.

That the definition of philosophy as the realization of the mind-base might seem odd to some is understandable. But it means that the definition at once expresses the goal of existence, that the perennial question, "What is philosophy?" is answered through a further question, "What is the goal of philosophy?" It further means that, since the realization of the mind-base is the approach toward that goal, the goal and method are one and the same. In fact, it would be anomalous should the goal and method not be identical. This meaning of philosophy is lacking in Western philosophy, a fact which becomes the source for the confusion in Western thought. If, however, philosophy were to trace itself back to Greek thought in the practical application of knowing thyself, then it would inevitably arrive at the realization of the mind-base. It goes without saying that since the Buddha's enlightenment, by contrast, Buddhist philosophy has accepted this realization as the fundamental principle of the living process. In Western thought, though, there was a long period of time, beginning in the Medieval period, when philosophy was known as the handmaiden of religion. With the advent of the modern period and the dawning of the concept of freedom, freedom of thought eventually made way for philosophy to emerge as a practical expression of life. In consequence, although only a few centuries have passed since the beginning of real Western philosophy, it has a long history in the science of logic and metaphysics which reveal a unique character to the Western way of thinking.

On this very point, interestingly enough, there is no evidence of any strong ideological pressure brought on in Buddhism to change its course of development in its 2500–year history. Although Greek and Buddhist thought evidence certain remarkable similarities, in the case of Buddhism, the ambience of freedom was left intact throughout its development. In China and Japan, for instance, Buddhism has interacted with indigenous ideas many times on both the comparative and practical levels, and all of this has exhibited great national ideological diversity.

If a hundred years in the Christian era were to be considered a year, Buddhism would already be twenty-five years old, while modern Western philosophy would only be four or five years old. This is not to denigrate a philosophy because of its relatively short history, but, rather, it is to reexamine and correct any thinking that places undue Western superiority over everything at the expense of neglecting Eastern thought.

If the realization of the mind-base is philosophy itself and its essential nature is to philosophize, then the principle of cognition must indicate or express the truth of things. The principle is readily acceptable to all and should not be restricted simply as a philosophic principle; in fact, it is a truth that belongs to the whole of natural science and is consonant with the nature of mathematics and geometry. In consequence, I firmly believe that it must be expressed in a unique diagram of the mind-base, as will be done shortly.

The reason for the inclusion or supplementation of the diagram on 'intuitive unconsciousness' is as follows. There are in man the realms of 'enlightenment and nonenlightenment,' as well as the confrontation between 'good and evil'." The existence of such realms in all beings is due to the identical and fundamental structure of the mind-base. Furthermore, with the nature of a synthetic judgment in its structural origins, there is in man's cognition that portion which directly reflects, as a camera does, the object of perception, and, at the same time, there is also that portion of the noncognitive realm of unintentional unconsciousness. The latter is the nature of 'intuitive unconsciousness'.

In the East, from olden days there were theories on the original goodness and original evilness of man which, in their train, have brought about extremely complicated argumentations. But, if such theories were to be accepted at all, then from the outset it would seem that the question of education and educability could not be taken up. Human beings actually cannot be typecast into any of the theories. Rather than any theory, in Buddhism it is asserted that all beings are endowed with 'Buddha-nature' (i.e., a nature that is the ground for the enlightened state of existence) and that only a portion (i.e., the portion relative to synthetic judgment or emptiness of *prajñā*-wisdom) of it refers to 'intuitive unconsciousness', and the other portions are still enmeshed in the grasping for a 'self' (*ātman*) and the attachment to 'unclear existence' or 'ignorance' (*avidyā*). The above analysis is depicted in the diagram of 'intuitive unconsciousness.'

Next come the steps involved in explaining the diagrams. But, if philosophy is the realization of the mind-base, then the diagrams themselves would be best shown in the light of a methodology. The reason for this is that speech is entirely conventional, being communicable only by way of the ear. Ordinarily, it is better to see something with respect to its existence as opposed to its nonexistence, and, therefore, it would serve best to use the diagram in a combined (ear-eye) sense. I have, so far, merely stated the locus of my own philosophy. At no time am I asserting that the diagrams depict absolutely unchanging truths. For, each of us must philosophize on his own and experience his own method. In so doing, one either is in accord with the diagrams or will improve on them. This is the essential ingredient in the methodology of comparative philosophy; indeed, it is the true function of philosophy itself.

In Buddhism from earlier days, intelligence was considered under three rubrics, namely, listening, thinking, and practicing. Yet nowadays, it is becoming fashionable to uncritically accept Western thought in translation and to indulge in valuation based merely on what is new or old. If truth, on the other hand, is the realization of the mind-base, then I feel that such a way of valuation should not be a part of the task of a philosopher. Should that not be the case, however, then clearly the philosopher does not know what the function of philosophy is. If the diagram of the mind-base agrees with one's own so-called diagrammatic philosophizing, then it would be quite easy to detect whether one's speech has arrived at self-realization or is the result of mere accumulation of knowledge. A true philosopher must not only apply his listening power of knowledge but also engage in the philosophizing method of listening and practice.

In sum, the diagram of the mind-base is thoroughly a methodology, the test of which can only be made by the application of thinking and practice by each individual alone. But, in the ultimate sense, it can have final determination on its own merits only when comparative investigations by all philosophies and disciplines have collaborated. It cannot simply be achieved by an individual or two and must always remain open as the path to be taken in future comparative thought and philosophy.

I am not merely criticizing present day philosophy, for I firmly believe that its important mission is to nourish the vision of understanding the nature of man and that it must, in essence, be viable and constantly cater to the practical demands of society.

The main themes of Kantian philosophy are twofold: (1) How is synthetic judgment possible? and (2) The nature of epistemic subjectivism. Now, it would seem to me that the requirements of these themes can be easily resolved by the singular concept of 'realization of the mind-base' which, in turn, would eliminate the necessity of engaging in such an abstruse thesis as the 'critique of pure reason.' In consequence, to engage in comparative thought without first clearly defining the nature of thought and philosophy, merely pitting one idea against another in the East-West context, would end in fruitless activity just as it has done in the past. Comparative thought is the science of thought process which is nothing but the function of philosophy, carrying with it its meaning and methodology. Philosophy, in this way, will be established on firm grounds.

Diagram of the Mind-base in East-West Context

As described by Kant, there is a fixed cognitive form in man's subjectivity. This form is comparable to our diagram of the mind-base, but, without realizing it, it would not be possible to understand the nature of man. In other words, the realization of the mind-base refers in reality to the simultaneous realization of man himself, thereby issuing forth the true meaning of epistemology. Kantian epistemology, in brief, asserts that the senses first intuitively grasp the object, next the pure forms of understanding categorize the object, and finally the active faculty of reason integrates the object. This analysis, I fear, shows that the diagram of the mind-base has not been realized and that the very dogmatism that Kant tried to avoid, in turn, ended in another dogmatic assertion. As he recognized intuitively that there is a fixed cognitive form in man's subjectivity, it would seem only proper that he should have pursued the search for a diagram of the cognitive form, a basis of cognition, upon the success of which the problem of the possibility of a synthetic judgment would have been solved automatically.

It may be thought that the quest for the diagram of the mind-base is very difficult, but it is not necessarily so. That is to say, although the structure of the mind-base cannot be seen at all, it nevertheless appears constantly in the form expressed by way of ordinary speech, i.e., it can be obtained and observed in our everyday conversations. By way of various expressions, it would not be difficult to intimate this unique structure, which is, paradoxical as it may seem, the very foundation of those expressions. To know the limits, realm, and construct of the mind-base constitutes the nature of epistemology. Thus the quest for the diagram of the mind-base must be the proper approach to epistemology. It would be extremely rare to find the above approach in Western philosophy from the Medieval period on, since it was under the spell of the metaphysical understanding of things; moreover, anything approaching the mind-base (i.e., its diagram) probably could not be found anywhere.

In comparison, Buddhist philosophy always begins with the truth of existence realized by Śākyamuni, the Buddha, in which the diagram of the mind-base was expressed as the Dharma of interrelational origination (*pratītya-samutpāda*). Moreover, this Dharma has evolved into the concepts of nirvāṇa, non-self (*anātman*), and impermanence (*anitya*), hoisting the banner of the Three Representative Marks of Buddhism or, by adding the concept of suffering (*duḥkha*), to constitute the Four Representative Marks. In time, the Mahāyāna tradition gradually clarified this diagram, and, by the time of the *Awakening of Faith in the Mahāyāna* (circa 6–7th century A.D.), it took on specific and minute dimensions such that it could be schematized.

Since our aim here is to focus on the methodology in East-West philosophy, the central problem lies in fleshing out any discord, as well as concord, between the fundamental nature in East-West philosophy and the fundamental diagram of the brain or cerebrum given to man as a unique natural gift. The future of comparative philosophy should be one that concentrates on how thinking is possible and how any development is possible, based on this fundamental diagram. This is not a problem of mere analysis but one that deals with the extremely fundamental nature of integration or synthesis. It is a problem of understanding the diagram involved in cognition and the realization of the mind-base.

In a sense, it can be said that even Kant had an inkling of this problem of the mind-base, but he did not pursue it further in terms of the structural nature germane to the truth of existence, i.e., the Buddhist Dharma. Thus, he suddenly shifted from the unconscious to the conscious realm and ended up in the pursuit of a discriminative type of knowledge based on a methodology of epistemological subjectivism.

However, to transcend all conscious elements within the immediacy of the moment is to grasp the nature of 'intuitive unconscious.' In Buddhist terminology, this phenomenon refers to the realm of both enlightenment and nonenlightenment, the latter also known as ignorance (*avidyā*). In engaging in comparative philosophy, it is essential to classify the realm of existence in this manner. Needless to say, there are many diverse views, each based on its own viewpoint thus complicating the comparative aspect. It would facilitate matters and comparisons should these views be classified into the singular realm of both enlightenment and nonenlightenment. This is, indeed, my feelings about instituting a new methodology in comparative philosophy.

How then can we seek the diagram? It would be best to return to the original nature of the self in order to raise and answer the following question: "From what standpoint do I think about things, and how do I express myself?" As it is quite plain to all, we always think and express ourselves from three standpoints: (1) subjective, (2) objective, and (3) synthesis, or the integration of (1) and (2). There is no other standpoint. It would not be inaccurate to view the structure of the human brain as similarly designed. To speak from the subjective standpoint, for example, does not mean to exclude the structure of the brain derived from the other two standpoints, for, as one is focused on, the other two remain in the background. The truth of the matter is that, in turn, each standpoint takes either centerstage or backstage. In the *Kegon Sūtra* (*Hua-yen Ching*), this phenomenon is expressed as follows: "the three realms are merely one mind." Thus, the structure, as a structure, is always in the nature of an unborn and undestructive entity, having been in man in this manner from time immemorial. The structure is expressed thus:

integrated or
synthetic nature

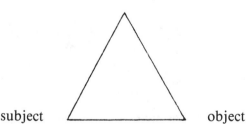

subject   object

The three realms constitute the structure of the brain or mind, and this seems to be the only way in which to observe the function. This diagram may well illustrate the basic scheme of Kant's

(*It would do well to keep in mind that diagrams in and of themselves do not make reality, nor do they come anywhere close to it. The author resorts to diagrams as mere representations of how the mind-base and intuitive unconsciousness function — Trans.*)

epistemic subject. Expressed by words, however, it becomes the familiar Buddhist denotation: "One mind, two aspects and three perspectives."[2]

The 'one mind', needless to say, refers to the structure of the mind or may even be interpreted as the 'locus' of cognition. For example, just as we face the camera at an object to take a snapshot, each and every shot taken depicts the 'one mind' or the 'locus' of cognition. In such a way, the 'one mind' functions repetitively and continuously to create unlimited phases of units, types, and classes.

The 'two aspects' refer to the synthetic (integrative) and analytic (independent) functions of the three components — subject, object, and synthesis of the two. In the case of synthetic judgment, all three components are integrated in the manner of simultaneous mutual penetration. In the case of analytic function, these components alternate being at centerstage and backstage, and, in any particular instance, one of them would appear prominently. In Buddhism, this is referred to as "the mind, Buddha and sentient creatures are not differentiated." In consequence, even Kant's epistemic scheme, if expressed geometrically, in all probability would be triadically constituted and would be close to the Buddhist expression of "one mind, two aspects and three perspectives." Furthermore, when these components function synthetically, they would resolve the initial problematic posed in Kant's *Critique of Pure Reason*, the searching question, "How is the a priori synthetic judgment possible?"

Kant was quite correct in pointing out that philosophy up to his time did not develop the notion of a synthetic judgment, and this fact generated a host of errors. Pursuing his words, it would seem that Western philosophy lacked the diagram for synthetic judgment, as well as for intuitive synthetic, and, accordingly, was found wanting in an epistemology based on a true structural nature of things.

Buddhist texts, on the other hand, are replete with reference to concepts that express the 'realization of the mind-base' or the structural nature of the mind as shown in the aforementioned "one mind, two aspects and three perspectives." Western philosophy does not have these, and thus Kant's critique is justified. His keen perception of the status of Western philosophy alone makes him a truly great philosopher. It can be surmised, moreover, that, had he known Buddhism, his philosophy would have developed in a different and more comprehensive way. Having the above discussion in view, it would not be proper to brand Buddhism as a form of mentalism or spiritualism in accordance with Western ways of thinking; indeed, it must be admitted that Buddhism is truly grounded in epistemology and expresses a bona fide philosophy.

Within Buddhist texts, we can easily observe the following concepts relative to the expression of the inherent (intuitive) synthetic judgment.

From Early Buddhism:

1. three marks (impermanence, non-self and nirvāṇa)
2. twelve-linked interrelational origination
3. Fourfold Noble Truths and Eightfold Noble Path
4. homage to the three treasures (Buddha, Dharma, and Sangha)

From *Prajñāpāramitā Sūtras*:

1. emptiness (*śūnyatā*)
2. five *skandhas* (aggregates of being) are all empty
3. twelve-linked interrelational origination is empty

From *Kegon (Hua-yen, Avataṁsaka) Sūtra*:

1. three realms are merely one mind
2. no separate realm of dharma outside the mind
3. the mind, Buddha and sentient creatures are not differentiated
4. interrelational origination of the total realm of elements (*dharmadhātu*); interrelational origination in terms of illimitable and endless interpenetration of elements or realities

From *Awakening of Faith in the Mahāyāna*:

1. one mind, two aspects and three greatnesses
2. interrelational origination "caused" by thusness (*tathatā*).[3]

There are indeed countless other citations available, but suffice it to say that, just by observing the above alone, one is made aware of the need and importance of comparative philosophy. In texts known as the jewels of Buddhist philosophy, e.g., the *Awakening of Faith in the Mahāyāna*, there is a natural and distinct epistemology which even, for example, Kant's problematics on God's existence, i.e., the proof of His metaphysical nature, can be resolved within the Buddhist doctrine of Three Bodies — the Body of Principle (*Dharmakāya*), Body of Transformation (*Nirmaṇakāya*) and Body of Bliss (*Sambhogakāya*) — which delineate a diagrammatic representation of the epistemological realm. Furthermore, the three idealized Kantian quests, namely, (1) a philosophy based on the nature of man, (2) a philosophy not in conflict with science, and (3) the establishment of the science of metaphysics, have all been fulfilled in Buddhism.

It seems so odd that Western philosophy, lacking the fundamental basis of the realization of the mind-base, starts with certain hypotheses and ideologies and then goes on confidently to discourse on the same problems, such as, God, man and the world, in East-West philosophy. It must be recognized that the common denominator in East-West thought is man himself, his intuitive grasp of the diagram of the mind-base. But then there is a parting of the way in the East and West in terms of whether the focus is on the conscious or unconscious realm. The latter realm naturally refers to the 'intuitive unconscious', the unique feature of Eastern philosophy.

A huge gulf may be created between metaphysics and epistemology in East-West philosophy based on whether the same structure of the mind-base is known and research is systematically carried out or whether it is taken merely as an image to pursue other interpretations, metaphysically speaking. It should be kept in mind, however, that a metaphysics without epistemology cannot be established, and, in the same vein, an ontology without epistemology cannot be established. These two disciplines cannot be separated and therein, I firmly believe, lies the linkage and possibility of comparative philosphy.[4]

Space and Time as Modes of Intuition

The senses, according to Kant, have the potential of intuitive representation, and the forms that give order to our sense perception are provided a priori within the senses themselves. He concluded that these forms are space and time. They do not exist independent of the senses as special entities but are a priori forms that condition the subject in each and every perception. And yet, Kant's theory of space and time as intuitive forms has neither complete necessity nor positive proof, and it seems to be merely another of his dogmatic stands. The reason for this critique is that there is immediate confusion in his philosophy. To expand, since the structure of the brain (i.e., diagram of the mind-base) is inherent in functions of all disciplines, it will not suffice to apply the structure only to philosophy, but with it there must be the possibility of doing mathematics or even understanding the principles of economics and political science. For the rule that governs the basis for the realization of the mind-base is also the rule that governs the basis of the theory of structure ('structuralism').

There are two basic errors in Kant's theory:

1. intuition functions only with respect to the senses, and
2. dimension of perception is limited by space and time.

We must presently explore these errors.

The first problem: There is no clear definition attached to the Kantian concepts of the sense, understanding, and reason. Lacking this, it would not be possible to compare them with Buddhist psychological conceptions, such as "the five aggregates of being (*pañca-skandhāh*) are all empty" or "the three realms are merely the mind."

The second problem: Although Kant claims that there is a kind of diagram (interpreted as having a structure) in the cognitive subject, why does he go on to give separate treatment to the functions of the senses, understanding, and reason and to completely leave out the important function of synthetic judgment? It seems that this would only engender analytic judgment and prevent the discovery of, or explorations into, the nature of synthetic judgment.

As an extension of the first problem, i.e, lacking clear definition of concepts, it would not be possible to establish a geometry based on such concepts as points, lines, and planes. As in calculation and algebra, it would also not be possible to establish anything by merely resorting to space and time.

Associated with the second problem, how would it be possible to separate the conceptual from the ontological? For it seems clear that intuition cannot be established through or by the senses alone. And yet, when one thinks, he already has in his thinking process the potential of separating the conceptual from the ontological. The reason for this is that there is a so-called structure of opposition inherent to the structural nature of the brains or intellect. But, if the basic structure of the intellect is limited to Kantian space and time, there will then arise the obstacles and confusion, as mentioned earlier. In order to prevent this from occurring, it is necessary, I believe, to include in the triadic relationship (senses, understanding, and reason) not merely space and time but a dimension that covers the total realm of the intellect. This can be illustrated in the following diagram.

Diagram 1-1

Western Psychological Analysis

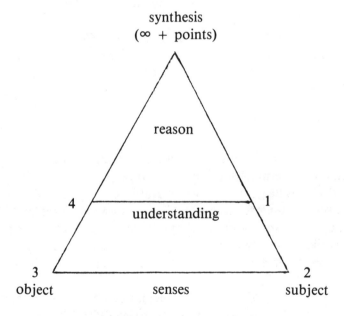

Note: The numbers depict dimensions (realms)

In the above sketch, there are dimensions with similar features, for example, the following:

a. on absolute dimension and points....dimensions with position and without size.
b. on time and lines....dimensions with mere length and without width
c. on two-dimensional and three-dimensional natures.... dimensions with surface features and solidity.

Considered in the above manner, there is a definite concurrence with the aforementioned Buddhist assertions, "the five *skandhas* are all empty" and "the three realms are merely mind", creating a situation which makes way for easy corroboration or verification of East-West comparative analysis. Let us expand on this in the next diagram which utilizes the notion that the five *skandhas* are empty. The five *skandhas* are corporeality (*rūpa*), feeling (*vedanā*), thought or imagery (*samjñā*), activity (*samskāra*), and consciousness (*vijñāna*).

Diagram 1-2

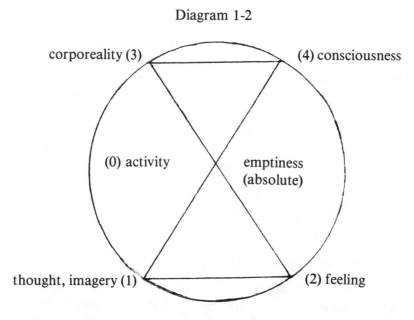

The above diagram, when folded from top to bottom, results in exactly the same triadic structure seen in Diagram 1-1. Considered in this light, Eastern thought (i.e., the Buddhist *skandhic* psychological analysis) and Western thought (i.e., the senses, understanding, and reason) are in general agreement, especially so if, as elaborated in the next diagram, it could be interpreted in the Buddhist context of "One Mind, Two Aspects and Three Perspectives." Moreover, it can be thought of as the structure of the mind-base which provides the unifying order to the dimensions themselves.

Diagram 1-3

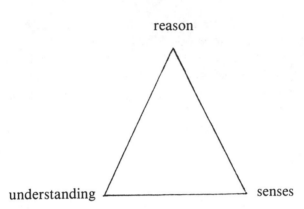

reason

understanding   senses

Viewed again from the standpoint of dimensions and considered as a structure of man's intellect, there will be a separation into top and bottom dimensions, in accordance with whether the right and left brains function independently or in combination. Consequently, the three standpoints relative to the senses, understanding, and reason must each, dimensionally speaking, be considered to have dual dimensions in the unique nature of 'contradictory self-unity.' This can be shown in the following diagrammatic representation:

reason = ∞ + points (transcendence)
understanding.....4 + 1 (time)
senses.....3 + 2 (space)

Note: numbers represent dimensions as shown in Diagram 1-1.

Considered in the above manner, the diagram of the mind-base creates an East-West rapprochement that had not been the case in the past. If considered, however, in the context of the realization of the mind-base, even such disciplines as plain geometry, which cannot work out problems in the framework of time and space, will be conceivable. Moreover, it will be possible to understand and explain the basis for the rise of Kantian antinomies, endless disputes (e.g., sophistry), and Zeno's paradoxes. Finally, it will be possible to understand that the basis of cognition beyond space will not function temporally and three-dimensionally when limited to the sight of only one eye.

Seen from another standpoint, the problem of interpreting such matters as subject and object or epistemology and ontology will loom large in future philosophical undertaking. As we are presently explaining things from the basic standpoint of realizing the mind-base, the so-called subject and object are provided inherently in the perceptual apparatus as such. Therefore, within the cognitive process, there is no simple subject viewing an object in the naive realistic sense.

It is quite consistent in Buddhism, therefore, to witness the appearance of the doctrine of "consciousness-only without external phenomena," i.e, there is only the configuration of the conscious realm and no external objects in and of themselves that impinge on the conscious mind. This doctrine belongs to the Yogācāra-vijñānavāda tradition which comes after the period of *prajñāpāramitā* philosophy. It does not necessarily deny the existence of the external world as such but only points to the fact that the subjective and objective spheres are inherent to cognition itself. When we examine the perceptual situation carefully, it becomes quite clear that objects or things do not exist in the mind, just as they do not exist in instruments, such as, in a microscope or TV set, both of which merely transmit the images of the objects themselves. Consequently, if philosophy were to be defined as the "study of the mind-process" or "knowing thyself," then it would invariably have to be the realization of the mind-base, the intimations with the Dharma (truth of existence), and the attainment of this unique "consciousness-only without external phenomena." If this were so, then the establishment of materialism and metaphysics would be possible only with a truly proper type of epistemology, and without this epistemology both ontology and metaphysics would collapse. Furthermore, any distinction between the concepts of good and evil would have to be lodged in the doctrine of One Mind and that all social structures would be mere reflections of this Mind. In consequence, it would be a grave misunderstanding to conclude naively that, just because the animal world is governed by the theory of evolution, the structure of human society must also conform to some type of social evolution.

I certainly do not wish to leave the impression that the diagram of the mind-base can be structured only in the manner presented, nor do I wish to assert that the structure retains a permanent, unchanging form. As philosophy must clearly be grounded in epistemology with definite function of the intuitive synthetic judgment, it can be asserted that all questions or problems must be oriented in such a way that the diagram of the mind-base is crystallized or fulfilled. Although in the past no geometric representation had been done with respect to this type of diagram, it is important to project such a representation so long as the source of the mind (mind-base) is central to cognition. This would represent, I believe, the most precise element in the methodology of comparative philosophy for, as discussed earlier, the resort to merely time and space in perception has failed to establish the cognitive realm.

In sum, then, we have introduced the Kantian critique of epistemology (i.e., the possibility of an a priori synthetic judgment) as a takeoff point in order to compare it with elements of basic psychology in Buddhism (i.e., the realization of the mind-base). It was also argued that Buddhism from the early period and through the Mahāyāna tradition had already resolved the problem of epistemology by its original discovery of and focus on the mind-base. The need to philosophize in the Kantian sense thereby has been rendered redundant.

Evidences of Intuitive Unconscious

I would now like to exhibit a few evidences on the reality of the nature of 'intuitive unconscious.' As my own comparative method is based on the rather simple realization of the mind-base and its nature of intuitive unconscious, and, acknowledging the fact that a structural diagram of the mind cannot be shown directly, I have done some research and constructed a diagram based on comparatively reliable data collected from various sources, such as, from literature, medicine, geometry, mathematics, and the like. There is, in consequence, no alternative but to directly apply and test the method with respect to each and every philosophical system. On account of this, revisions may have to be made to parts of the diagram, or a better explanation may have to be found. On my part, since I do not regard the diagram as absolute, I anticipate such revisions and explanations. Moreover, it should be clearly understood that I did not discover the method, since the realization of the mind-base had been prevalent and expounded in the various Buddhist texts from the beginning. Yet, I remain confident with a singular unshakable faith that the realization of the mind-base lies at the core of philosophical methodology.

The label "intuitive unconscious" is my own, one that cannot be traced to any text, but it is an important aspect of consciousness that cannot be excluded from the methodology. The reason for this is that, by realizing the mind-base, man becomes enlightened (*satori*), manifesting the Buddha-nature, and naturally clarifies the nature of good (*zen*). In searching through Buddhist texts, however, it is difficult, if not impossible, to locate a clear and direct explanation on the realization of the mind-base concerning the question of evil (*aku*). But in philosophy we are earnest about knowing the direct connection of this mind-base to the nature of good and evil. It is not sound philosophical explanation to merely assert that they arise from ignorance (*avidyā*) or defilement (*kleśa*). In such texts as the *Awakening of Faith in the Mahāyāna*, the phenomenon is explained thus: "The so-called mind-nature is always without base or evil thought and therefore known as unchanging. On account of nonattainment of the singular Dharma realm of existence, there is nonconformity to the mind and a sudden rise of evil thought which is known as ignorance."[5]

The passage on the "sudden rise of evil thought" is a famous one, but, since it is a religious statement, which in itself is fine, it will not do in the field of philosophy which requires a more precise universal nature of explanation. I have therefore examined the diagram of the mind-base by seeking out corresponding ideas, such as, the '*prajñā*-emptiness' (emptiness derived through wisdom) with the synthetic judgment, or, in the case of the equation, the reference not merely to numbers and symbols but to the notion of zero which functions intuitively and in an unconscious way as it is grasped conventionally by ordinary people. This so-called unconscious common sense function of synthetic judgment is seen as corresponding to 'intuitive unconscious', which, in turn, is directly related to the realization of the mind-base, as well as to the basis of judgment on the nature of good and evil.

I would now like to demonstrate the existence of the 'intuitive unconscious.' Since philosophy in the past rarely, if ever, considered this demonstration, it existed merely as an idea and did not become a legitimate pursuit. It would seem that a feature of contemporary philosophy is an overemphasis on logic without offering precise meaning to even a single concept. This may be one of the reasons for the difficulty in understanding philosophy, but the difficulty is not without a basis.

Demonstration 1-1

Goblet and Profile (1921)

The above diagram, belonging to Edgar J. Rubin, is famous in psychology, but, since psychology is, in general, a descriptive science, it does not explain the causes of the phenomena but examines only their existence. There are, of course, many other illusionary examples to be found in the field of psychology. Suffice it to say that, from my perspective of the realization of the mind-base, the above diagram is a prime example of exhibiting the nature and existence of the 'intuitive unconscious.' That is to say, by looking at a thing with geometric, plane, or three-dimensional features, one sees its so-called shape. But, in reality, one cannot see a shape in and of itself because one must rely on the surrounding space or emptiness to observe the shape as a shape, just as, for example, shapes and figures on an artist's canvas materialize owing to the background. Rubin's diagram is then a special instance where it is interesting to note that new interest and meaning are aroused by the perceptual reaction to the mutually suggestive background. In psychological terms, a structure is provided by the unique concept of *'prajñā*-emptiness' in Buddhism and by the concept of a 'mathematical zero' which is not to be interpreted as a literal 'nothing.' In other words, the phenomenon of seeing something indicates the full display of intuitive unconscious within the function of realizing the mind-base. This would seem very ordinary, but, in truth, it is in philosophy a most important key to the resolution of such matters as the proof of God's existence, settling endless disputes, or understanding problems related to the nature of enlightenment (*satori*). The concepts of *'prajñā*-emptiness' and 'zero' are undeniably important for the understanding of problematics in philosophy and the natural sciences.

On December 8th, at the moment the 35-year old Śākyamuni saw the morning star, he attained the realm of *satori* which at once was the discovery of emptiness, of peace and nirvāṇa, marking the beginning of the quest for the realization of the Buddhist Dharma. Both Rubin's diagram and Śākyamuni's *satori* point at the similar nature of manifestation and may well be treated alike. In other words, one manifestation in the area of psychology and the other in philosophy and religion have greatly contributed to their respective developments. As manifested phenomena, they can be seen and treated in the same vein as revealing a structure of the cognitive base. The fact that there was neither mathematics nor a developed form of script during Śākyamuni's times makes it all the more astounding that a principle of universal truth of existence was so dramatically discovered and has continued to hold sway for the past 2500 years.

The *prajñā*-emptiness and mathematical zero which easily incline toward the intuitive unconscious are actually, from the dimensional standpoint, the 'antinomical self-identity' of the zero and the infinite. It is for this reason that I have expressed the diagram of the mind-base in terms of zero and infinity $(0 + \infty)$ in synthetic judgment.

In Demonstration No. 1-2, the point is the intersection of the two coordinates, and, although planes X and Y depict infinity, ordinarily the voidness (*mu*) aspect remains uncognized. That is, it is all too often that the singular, double, curve, and straight line are readily cognized, while the initial vital point of activity for the great foundation of the mind as emptiness (*kū*; *śūnyatā*) or

Demonstration 1-2

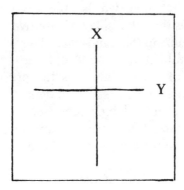

Coordinate axis

voidness (*mu*) goes uncognized. By ignoring this vital point, all of analytic geometry becomes impossible.

It should be emphasized that the initial vital point of emptiness and zero is definitely not in the nature of a nonbeing in opposition to a being. This unique nature in perception in Buddhism is referred to as "truly empty wondrous being" (*shinkū-myō-u*).

Were we to go to extremes to characterize formally what the nature of truth is, it would be as follows: What is, is, and what is not, is not. Yet, we know that our cognitive function does not determine matters of truth in such simplistic terms. We cannot, for example, swiftly pass judgment on the nature of a mathematical zero as to whether it is an entity or a nonentity. The reason for this is very simple. Without the zero, the whole run of numbers would not be possible. So, although it is said that God created the world *ex nihilo*, the assertion is problematic. As seen in Rubin's diagram, we shape or create things daily or from moment to moment within the nature of voidness (*mu*).

Demonstration 1-3

$$1 + 2 = 3$$
$$(1 + 2) - 3 = 0$$

The above equations, as everyone knows, are simple arithmetic operations, but they constitute at once the original form of all mathematical logic. For, to think genuinely is to reflect the original form of thinking of all human beings, and this form must be considered to express the structure of the mind-base. While the first equation $(1 + 2 = 3)$ is an example of intuitive synthetic judgment, the second $[(1 + 2) - 3 = 0]$ is the reflection of the first in terms of the nature of "mutuality of one and many" (*itta-sōsoku*).

Considering the matter carefully, however, the first question is normally spoken of as a function of dialectic, and the second, the necessity of mutual penetration of individuality and totality. But both fulfill the structure of the same mind and differ only in their respective function. Based on the realization of the mind-base, Eastern logic differs entirely from Western formal logic. The zero, as seen from the earlier diagram of the mind-base, is the synthetic judgment, as well as the locus of the whole equation. It is also referred to as constituting the nature of the One Mind, the locus of the total perception. These two equations are then seen within the structure of the aforementioned "One Mind, Two Aspects and Three Perspectives." The 'locus of emptiness' is necessary for the first equation. In the case of the second equation, if it does not come to a zero (i.e., if individuality and totality are not mutually penetrative), the first equation is either faulty or nonestablished. The important point for all to remember is that we should seriously think of the zero to be so vitally important that its absence will stymie all operations. The zero is in the form of the intuitive unconscious and cannot be ignored by merely lapsing into thinking that everything is all right since it already has served its purpose in the operation.

Furthermore, if the way of thinking based on the realization of the mind-base is taken as a form of dialectic, then the first and second equations would probably be a form of dialectical logic. In the *Awakening of Faith in the Mahāyāna*, this is expressed in the following way:

> *One and many mutually penetrate;*
> *Being and Nonbeing mutually penetrate;*
> *Expressed by words, it is the condition of true thusness*
>   (tathatā).

The dialectical logic of *Madhyamaka Śāstra* probably delves into the nature of things in the order of the second equation, $[(1 + 2) - 3 = 0]$. We normally perceive only the formal aspects, thinking merely in formal terms, e.g., accepting the Hegelian triadic thesis, antithesis, and synthesis as the only valid form of dialectic. But this is a very narrow view, as seen from the Eastern standpoint.

It is often said that the East did not develop logic. Yet it should be noted that the development of logic does not necessarily follow directly with the movement in rationalism alone. For example the logic of *prasanga* (systematic critique of views) found in Nāgārjuna's *Madhyamaka Sāstra* can be referred to as a form of dialectic, but it would be very difficult to determine and establish its formal nature. In the ultimate sense, it is based on the realization of the mind-base and is definitely a method which leads to true understanding by correcting the errors committed as the dialogue proceeds.

Although it is asserted that the discovery of the zero in mathematics in India came late, probably in the fifth to sixth century A.D., the fact that there are many elements of mathematical logic in Buddhist logic which antedates the above discovery by several centuries at least attests to the presence and function of the realization of the mind-base and the nature of *prajñā*-emptiness.

In Buddhism, the realization of the mind-base (corresponding to the realm of *satori* or enlightenment) and the nature of intuitive unconscious (corresponding to the realm of *mayoi* [nonenlightenment = ignorance, *avidyā*]) are seen in the manner presented in the following chart.

The chart below gives a bird's-eye view of the realms of enlightenment and nonenlightenment in the Buddhist and Western psychological traditions, whereby the former refers to the nature of *satori* as a result of the realization of the mind-base, and the latter shows up the psychological nature of intuitive unconscious which encompasses the whole run of perception. In the former, when the *ālaya-vijñāna* (storehouse consciousness) is transformed into the Wisdom of the Great Round Mirror, reflecting all thoughts as they are without discrimination, there will be *satori* which is also the state of manifesting Buddha-nature in all beings, a nature depicting the potentiality of shifting to the enlightened realm of existence.

Realms of Enlightenment (*satori*) and Nonenlightenment (*mayoi*)

Vijñānavāda Thought ('Consciousness-only' School)		Western Thought (psychology)
		Dimensions
immediate internal-external bond (corporeality, *rūpa*)	— denial of common sense realism	
five sense faculties (sensitivity, feelings, *vedanā*) (the five senses are all sense consciousnesses)	— wisdom developed to transcend defiled elements in the senses . . . . five senses	----intuition $(3 + 2)$
sixth consciousness (thought, imagery, *saṃjñā*) (*mano-vijñāna*)	— wisdom developed to transcend defiled elements in the sixth consciousness . . . . understanding	----space and time context $(4 + 1)$
seventh consciousness (mental activity, discrimination, *saṃskāra*) (*manas*)	— wisdom developed to transcend dichotomous nature in the thought process . . . . reason	synthesis or integration 'locus' of perception $(\infty + \text{point})$
eighth consciousness (receptable or storehouse consciousness, *vijñāna*) (*ālaya-vijñāna*)	— wisdom developed to reflect all forms of thought as they are . . . . intuitive unconsciousness (conventional nature of truth, *saṃvṛti-sat*)	

(Note: These four wisdoms finally transform the eight-consciousnesses into the enlightened state of existence.)

(Note: This is the realm of the rise of antinomies in Western philosophy)

Demonstration 1-4

Although it was stated earlier that there is a lack of definition in Western philosophy, we find an exception in Friedrich Engels who fostered and gave us a definition of materialism (naturalism). How are we to cope with this situation? Let me qualify my earlier statement by saying that I did not assert categorically that there is no definition in Western philosophy, but, rather, there is no definition proferred to the question, "What is philosophy?" In this sense, does Engels's definition of materialism answer that question? Engels made the following assertion:[6]

> The great fundamental question in the whole of philosophy, particularly contemporary philosophy, is the question of the relationship between thought and existence . . . What is the original source . . . mind or nature (matter)?

On the basis of how the question is posed and answered, we have philosophers who have been divided into the two camps of idealism and materialism (naturalism). The materialistic (naturalistic) definition is still current today, and there are not a few philosophers who believe in it fervently and perhaps blindly. Viewed from the standpoint of comparative methodology, however, its analysis of things is still within the realm of intuitive unconsciousness (nonenlightened realm), consisting of arbitrary judgment, and thus without true philosophical foundations. This can be seen clearly in the following diagram.

relationship (synthesis)

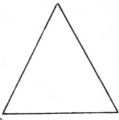

thought (understanding)   existence (senses)

(Note: Epistemology considered central to philosophy)

The content of the first half of Engels's thesis is expressed in the above diagram. The latter half, however, i.e., the question posed, has changed into something new and can be expressed as follows.

unconscious (relationship)

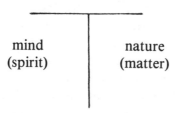

mind   nature
(spirit)   (matter)

(Note: An ontology based on a dyadic opposition)

What Engels means, in consequence, is that, while sensing the fundamental question in philosophy as an epistemology that involves the intuitive synthetic judgment initially, it turns suddenly into the nature of unconscious and changes into a dyadic opposition between thought and existence. In short, his *intellectus* (synthetic judgment) has immediately become the unconscious and shifted to analytic judgment, presenting a prime example of the intuitive unconsciousness.

Viewed from the Buddhist standpoint, the above depicts the manner of thinking of the average person who does not have any philosophical leaning but whose nature of thinking is considered to fall into the category of ignorance (*avidyā*) or truth on the conventional level. But, one who is able to avoid the trappings of the conventional function of truth is considered to be on the way to the enlightened state.

The nature of the enlightened (*satori*) and nonenlightened (*avidyā*) realms describes generally speaking, the difference between Eastern and Western approaches. Eastern philosophy can be called, summing up from what we have discussed at length so far, a type of 'psychological structuralism'. Western philosophy, by contrast, is logically oriented and deviates from the Eastern orientation. Western logic, furthermore, as stated earlier, lacks the synthetic judgment, i.e., is without real inductive method, and must always remain a logic functioning on the basis of dyadic opposition where the object is constantly in opposition to the subject. So despite the fact that the first half of Engels's statement constitutes a proper epistemology aimed at the realization of the mind-base, the latter half shows the statement reduced to a logic of alternatives. The sudden transformation from the intuition of the mind-base to the unconscious realm cannot be attributed solely to the influence of Christianity, for example, since the same phenomenon is equally true with respect to the Easterner who also thrives on common sense logicality of things.

Let us return to the main theme of philosophy. The object of investigation in philosophy has been said to be man, the science of man, i.e., to know thyself or to realize the mind-base. This is the fundamental teaching that runs through the whole of Buddhist philosophy from the Theravāda to Mahāyāna traditions. But the principle of the teaching is found in the very consciousness of ordinary man and even lies nascently in the logic used in Western philosophy in an 'unconscious conscious' way. In this sense, it was referred to as the realization of the mind-base, and its structure was expanded into the Buddhist "One Mind, Two Aspects and Three Perspectives," all of which is not, of course, easily realizable by everyone. The realization, however, is the goal of religion and education. In order to achieve it, namely to perfect the inner character of man, there are many steps involved. The basis for the various stages in man's character, despite having the same structure of the mind-base, lies in the manifestation of the intuitive unconscious. The realization of the mind-base, in Kantian terms, is the a priori synthetic judgment (intuitive synthetic judgment), a proper epistemology and function of the intuitive unconscious. In this way, it is possible to explain the rise of different stages in the character of human beings who function within the same structural context. In the *Awakening of Faith in the Mahāyāna*, the intuitive unconscious as stated earlier is referred to as the "sudden rise of evil thought." Since the reference is hardly to be taken as philosophical, what carries the meaning of being intuitive but at the same time without being conscious (while the image intuited is left unaffected) is phrased the 'intuitive unconscious.'

(*It might be profitable to pause here to sum up the discussion. First of all, the author is not against epistemology at all. What he is against is the false rise of dichotomous elements in the epistemic function whether, for example, it is Engels's definition of materialism and its consequence or Kant's a priori synthetic judgment. What is at stake here is the unwarranted way in which the elements are spoken of and treated within the context of* epistemology; in other words, these elements are taken to be *'realities'* which enable the process to proceed, whereas, in truth, the opposite seems to be the case. That is to say, the total context in which the elements are at play, rather than the elements themselves, should be taken into account from the very beginning. An error arises when the elements take on the dominant roles in the process. In order to upright the situation of the epistemic function, the author has gone into diagrammatic representations to exhibit the barren path taken and at the same time to show the way out of the situation. Thus, the use of diagrams as demonstrative devices has so-called therapeutic, as well as cathartic, values. They exhibit the problematic areas and structural natures that ought to be focused. In another demonstration, the author has introduced mathematical formulas to depict the way both Eastern and Western *'dialectical logic'* functions, especially with the introduction of the concept of zero. To his credit, the author has irrefutably shown that the simple equations, $1 + 2 = 3$ and $1 + 2 - 3 = 0$, have profound epistemic differences, the former is synthetic while the latter integrative or holistic, and both advance the epistemological function because of the inherently dialectical nature of the mind process. At this point, the author introduces the Buddhist concept of emptiness or, more specifically, 'prajñā-emptiness', an emptiness derivable only from the enlightened nature of things. What he has shown is that, structurally speaking and in a very indirect manner, the mathematical zero functions in an analogous way to the experience of prajñā-emptiness. This phenomenon shows the important link, not only in East-West understanding of each other but, more importantly, the proximity and, indeed, the coexistent nature of the conventional (unenlightened) and absolute (enlightened) realms of truth. — *Trans.)*

Logic East and West

In 1946, a year after the end of World War II, F.S.C. Northrop published *The Meeting of East and West. An Inquiry Concerning World Understanding*,[7] which can be considered to be the first systematic work in East-West comparative thought and culture in recent decades.[8] In it, he distinguishes between the aesthetic component and concept by postulation, and notes that Eastern thought is based on the former, and intuitive and Western thought, in contrast, is based on the latter and, therefore, is rationalistic. Since much of Eastern thought is grasped intuitively, it is undifferentiated and based on a continuum that dissolves differences. It would seem to me, however, that his theory is still overly antilogical and has other phases that are unacceptable. Be that as it may, as we now set out to engage in East-West comparative philosophy, we must first of all be cognizant of the fact that, historically, the West totally lacks understanding of synthetic judgment (*intellectus*) where its logic is based primarily on analytic judgment. Next, we must not view this logic uncritically as we introduce Eastern logic with a different historical background to examine the possibility and merits of any comparison.

Is it permissible to advance the concept by postulation for the sole reason that it conforms to the canons of logic, as Northrop asserts? Moreover, why is the intuited component undifferentiated and ungraspable? A strong feeling mounts that a wider discrepancy exists than formerly thought of, in regard to the perception of Eastern philosophy by Western philosophers. It is also felt that comparative thought, without a firm theoretical basis, would not be acceptable. Northrop, however, was entirely correct in pointing out the logical differences in Eastern and Western thought.

Reflecting on the matter further, it is true that Eastern (especially Buddhist) logic and Western logic have special features that mutually could be distinguished. Simply put, the difference is one of Western logicism (analytic judgment) and Eastern psychology (psychological structuralism = intuitive synthetic judgment = epistemology). So when the Westerner views Buddhist logic as characterized by the undifferentiated continuum which dissolves all distinctions, he has not actually experienced the intuitive synthetic judgment, which is unfortunate. It is, therefore, extremely difficult to explain the elements at play. I will attempt to do so by resorting to a short allegory. Since, in comparative philosophy, the treatment of Buddhist logic is inevitable, there is a need to understand the basis of divergence in Eastern and Western logic. This will be done by the use of diagrams derived from Buddhist philosophy.

The allegory is a famous one first presented by Vivekānanda at the World's Parliament of Religions in conjunction with the Chicago World Columbian Exposition in 1893. The allegory, "A

Frog in the Well Knows Nothing of the Great Ocean," runs as follows:

> A frog lived in an old well where he was born, grew up and con-
> tinued to live out his old age. Suddenly one day, another frog from
> the direction of the ocean leaped by and accidentally fell into the
> well.
> Old frog: "Where did you come from?"
> Visitor: "I came from the vicinity of the ocean."
> Old frog: "Is the ocean narrower or wider than this well?"
> Visitor: "Nonsense! There is no comparison between this tiny
>   narrow well and the great expansive ocean!"
> Old frog: "There is no place on earth wider and greater than this
>   well! You are a liar! Get out!"

The allegory ends here. The argument of course will not end no matter how long it goes on. It would end, however, if the two frogs were to go to the top of the hill to view at once the old well and the ocean.

The allegory clarifies much that has taken place in East-West comparative philosophy. It has done this by rendering so clear the comparative and structural aspects as if we were observing an experiment in a scientific laboratory.

The following Diagram 1 represents the Buddhist sketch of the situation and Diagram 2 the Western sketch.

Diagram 1

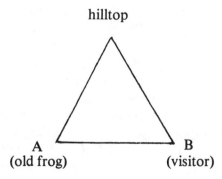

The diagram shows:
    (a) subject-object . . . . synthesis or integration effected
    (hilltop view)

(b) realization of mind-base = psychological structuralism . . . .
true epistemology (psychological substantiation or confirmation)

Diagram 2

ignorance (nonenlightenment; *avidyā*)

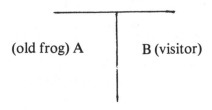

(old frog) A   B (visitor)

The diagram shows:
(a) dyadic opposition (intuitive unconscious)
(b) discriminative knowledge based on ratio = logicism . . . .
ontology (logical teleology).

Kant is a great philosopher who, nourished within the Western philosophical tradition, opened up the nature of the mind by an attempt to unify epistemology and metaphysics in terms of a scheme based on a so-called dialectic of the a priori. Actually, there is nothing ontological or structural to add to this scheme, as it encompasses the Buddhist psychological structuralism which depicts the realization of the mind-base. In Kant's analysis, however, we are able to discern the distinction between the epistemology of Eastern philosophy based on a theory of psychological substantiation and the metaphysics of Western philosophy based on a theory of logical substantiation. More importantly, though, his scheme — a scheme that focuses on the subject — should be fulfilled or consummated by East-West dialogues.

According to Kant, our consciousness is established by the synthesis of the senses and understanding which cannot be done without sense intuition (Diagram 2). Accordingly, it is necessary to have a synthesis of the a priori forms of space and time in the senses, as well as the a priori forms of understanding (categories of understanding), thus showing up the distinguishing characteristics of logicism and dimensionality. In other words, the categories merely compromised the spatial and temporal characters of phenomena and thereby exhibited the limited nature in man (i.e., Diagram 2 = discriminative knowledge). It just describes the consciousness of the phenomena only, not of the things themselves, as Kant readily admitted. If, however, man has another form of intuition, other than the one limited to the senses, i.e., if he has the power of intellectual intuition (*intellektuelle Anschauung* = Diagram 1), then his consciousness would be interpreted quite differently from what it is currently.

When the knowledge of the other form of intuition becomes a reality, we would be able to cognize things themselves. We would be able to grasp the nature of the Buddhist thusness (*tathatā*) of the mind. But this knowledge eludes us under the present understanding of man's cognitive process. For, although we conceivably can think of nonsensual intuition, namely intellectual intuition (Diagram 1), we cannot understand what it is, i.e., the nature of the intuitive unconsciousness. God, incidentally, probably employs intellectual intuition (i.e., Diagram 1 = realization of the mind-base = structuralism involving the One Mind, Two Aspects and Three Perspectives). By contrast, man ordinarily employs the only possible sense intuition (analytic judgment) and cannot transcend its limits, i.e., not being able to distinguish between *ratio* and *intellectus* cognition. We must, therefore, acknowledge the limits of our cognitive process and aim at the grasp of truth based on man's total locus of existence. And we would fail, indeed, were we to ignore the limits and attempt to expand on the cognitive process by seeking for elements outside the realm of the senses or phenomena.

Past metaphysics had indeed perpetuated this failure. It attempted to cognize transcendental (trans-sense) elements, such as, the soul, cosmology of the world, or the nature of God. Since matters of the senses are not understood experientially from the start, the emphasis shifted to a metaphysics of understanding based on the cognition of a priori transcendental elements. An a priori cognition, however, cannot be established. As indicated earlier, this shows up Kant's error in fostering the theory of time and space in epistemology. He did not notice the fact that the dimension of reason is identical to the dimension that functions like the mathematical zero. In the *Awakening of Faith in the Mahāyāna*, as seen earlier, this dimension is expounded by the nature of true thusness (*tathatā*), unencumbered by words, and depicted by the mutual penetration of being and nonbeing in the realm of Dharma (truth of existence). With Nāgārjuna, similarly, he elucidates on the same idea in the famous verses thus:[9]

> The teaching of the Dharma by the various Buddhas is based on two truths: namely, the relative (worldly) truth and the absolute (supreme) truth.

> Those who do not know the distinction between the two truths cannot understand the profound nature of the Buddha's teaching.

The Buddha's teaching is similar in dimension to the mathematical zero which is neither space nor time but without whose nature and function all operations cease. To be fair to Kant, he did however assert the shortcomings of past metaphysics. But then he sought to remedy the situation by applying the a priori categories of understanding beyond the senses, to the transcendental realm. So that although past metaphysics had erred, it did not happen fortuitously or by design. Its origins must be traced to the inevitable phenomenon which springs forth from the nature of man's inception of the cognitive process. The intellect of man, fundamentally, does not remain satisfied by mere intellectual consciousness but goes further to actually furnish the unifying element in the understanding. This is namely the function of reason. If understanding has the power of unifying phenomena based on certain rules, then reason, in turn, must have the power to unify and regulate understanding by its own rules. In other words, where understanding synthetically unifies the various phenomenal elements to establish experience, reason further synthesizes this understanding to issue forth the absolute cognitive unity. Granted that Kant's dialectic of the a priori proceeds on to other functions, the diagrams relative to the frog in the well have plainly expressed for us the basic difference in Eastern and Western methodology.

Western metaphysics went off its course early on. In the process, its nature of synthetic judgment was usurped by theology, its psychological structure limited to the framework of discriminative knowledge, its intuitive synthetic knowledge disappeared, and, finally, it was left with only the analysis of psychological structure of things. Consequently, there could be no recognition of intuitive synthetic judgment as found in Eastern philosophy, and, as with Kant, it fell into the delusory activity of establishing intuition of the senses. This denied the proper study of psychological structuralism by closing off the intuition of the mind-base, the result being a metaphysics of logicism sapped of true epistemology. That is not, of course, the proper road to the science of man. Interestingly enough, Kant compared the spectacular achievements in mathematics and the natural sciences and grieved that metaphysics was limited to groping in the dark. To know thyself was, after all, the basis of philosophy. But, since the realization of the mind-base which is central to the self was closed off to man by theological considerations (divine perogative), there was not a mote of a chance that philosophy as the science of man would have arisen and compelled Western philosophy to take a course other than the erroneous path it has taken for the last two thousand years.

The two diagrams relative to the frog in the well have functioned well to delineate the difference in the epistemology of Eastern thought (Buddhist philosophy) and the Kantian oriented thinking method within the Western philosophical tradition. In such a way, Kant's schemata succeeded in clarifying our goal of elucidating the Eastern approaches to things. That comparative philosophy works with such schemata indicates that, as a methodology, it is truly effective. The doctrine of One Mind, Two Aspects and Three Perspectives is a theory of structure. On the other hand, the diagram on the triadic subject, object, and synthesis of the two allows quite an effective comparative contrast between the synthetic judgment and the unconscious turned into the intuitive unconscious (= logicism = metaphysics) in the T-shaped Diagram 2. Finally, I feel that as a methodology of comparative philosophy it should, by all means, be given careful examination.

Recapitulation

Comparative philosophy and contrast of ideas

Eastern philosophy, in this instance represented by Buddhism which began with the inner conviction of truth realized by the historical Buddha, was later crystallized by four doctrinal marks—

impermancnce, non-self, nirvāna, and universal nature of suffer-ing. It maintained, through the Theravāda and Mahāyāna tradi-tions, a continuity of ideological development by concentrating on an epistemology based on the realization of the mind-base. Western philosophy, by contrast, has fused the essentials of Greek and Christian thought, setting aside the original doctrine and ad-monition of knowing thyself and coming to regard the philosophical enterprise to be in the domain of different areas of concentration, such as, epistemology, metaphysics, theism, atheism, materialism, and idealism, while neglecting all along the most important pursuit of unifying all the disciplines. In such a situation, the objective of comparative studies in the various areas of concentration would only end in contrast of ideas. There would always remain the crucial problem of seeking a singular meaning to what philosophy, in and of itself, is. It would be a goal of seek-ing a singular truth of existence. With the resolution of this prob-lem, however, it would then be possible to have a meaningful com-parative discourse in a single arena.

We have thus followed the following format. We first presented the definition of philosophy as the realization of the mind-base. What deviates from this realization was referred to as the intuitive unconscious. We then developed a theory of psychological struc-turalism, and, based on this theory, we concluded with a methodology of comparative philosophy.

Realization: holistic man versus individual

The nature of realization of true man has two components: in-tuitive synthetic judgment, and analytic judgment. These two components generally distinguish the meaning and consciousness relative to the enlightened nature of man and nonenlightened nature of the ordinary individual, an important distinction first ex-pounded by Tetsurō Watsuji in his, Ethics as the Study of Man.[10] That is to say, where enlightened man's realization is oriented in intuitive synthetic judgment, the ordinary individual's realization is in analytic judgment. The former is penetrative and complete with respect to total existence of man and the latter superficial and divisive in the quest of knowledge.

The theory of dual components is readily accommodated in Eastern philosophy, but that is not the case in the unclear state of

Western philosophy. For example, the concepts of freedom and self-realization of the individual are quite current today. Unfortunately, there is a vast difference in interpretation of them in the East and West. Again, there are different forms of democracy in the world, such as the American or even the early founding Soviet types, but there is no program to bring them all together, which suggests that the object of future comparative work may well entertain the unification of divergent points of view.

Weakness of Western epistemology

As illustrated in the allegory of the frog in the well, the projected frog on the hilltop depicts a man grounded in true realization and the frog in the well lacking synthetic judgment. In contemporary Western philosophy, since the time of the split of *nous* into *intellectus* and *ratio*, aside from the belief in God, there has been no realization of man qua man, i.e., man as a wholesome complete being. It must be reiterated that each person is endowed with the structure of the mind-base, but its true understanding could only be achieved by education geared toward an orientation in intuitive synthetic judgment. The structure, moreover, manifests as the intuitive unconscious in ordinary nonenlightened individuals, but it can be transformed by proper education. That is to say, within the realm of intuitive unconscious, the intuitive synthetic judgment must be realized. The realization of intuitive synthetic judgment depicts the capture of humanism, the highest state of manhood, the basis of true personality, and the establishment of the cornerstone of all social life. When the social order, oriented in logicism, is likened to that maintained by the frog in the well, competition or combativeness reigns, wherein the victor manages the vanquished, with a hierarchy established on the basis of superior and inferior, advantaged and disadvantaged, and so forth. On the other hand, when man stands on the foundation of realizing true manhood as typified by the frog on the hilltop, there will be a social order based on truth and righteousness.

It can be said that contemporary Western philosophy lacks an epistemology grounded in the intuitive synthetic judgment, one that is not geared toward the realization of the mind-base. Seen in this light, the Northropian analysis of the theoretic and intuitive components take on added meaning, i.e., it reveals the basic dif-

ference between Western metaphysics (based on logicism) and
Eastern epistemology. In the Buddhist context, the difference
shows up well in the exposition of the doctrine of twelve-linked interrelational origination which is interpreted at once in clockwise
movement (from ignorance to aging-death) and counterclockwise
(from aging-death to ignorance). This is not a paradox or an illogical phenomena. It actually points at the perception of things,
respectively, from the nonenglightened and enlightened standpoints. In the *Awakening of Faith in the Mahāyāna*, the same
phenomena are treated under the rubric of enlightenment and
nonenlightenment, as we have indicated earlier.

Philosophy is the very foundation of man's education and
should not be relegated to an ineffective discipline as it exists today. Should indiscriminate confusion persist between the realization of man qua man and the realization of egoistic individual, the
situation would then be comparable to the hilltop frog versus the
frog in the well, and the society in which we live forever would be
divided between peaceful and combative forces.

Man is born twice

Man belongs to the animal kingdom, but other animals, such as
the lion and tiger, are born and die as lion and tiger. Should man
be born and nourished as other animals, he would end up like the
rest of the animals without attaining true manhood. But man is
such a unique social creature that he owes it to himself *to be born
again in society*. In essence, this refers to social education and
character building — to creating a social livelihood and educational
excellence. To learn a language, form good habits, discipline
oneself, develop techniques, and so on, are all directed toward a
meaningful life in society. Accordingly, no primitive tribe is
without a religion, as all taboos, myths, and the like, relative to it
have the instructive prototype or model guided by basic principles.
Thus, all religious and educational systems must ally to form a
united front and move toward the same goal. In the long history of
man, however, we have witnessed the mutual antagonism among
religions which often flare up in open hostilities to disrupt the
cause of peace in the world. History shows that even religions have
been victimized by their own selfish designs and lose sight of the
larger dimensions of life, the synthetic judgment and realization of
true manhood. Although Northrop asserted that the Easterner's
life is involved in the intuitive aesthetic continuum, the realization

of man qua man can be a possibility only because each man has both the synthetic intuitive and analytic realms which he alone must activate to the fullest extent.

Man is prone, however, to become the frog in the well. To become the hilltop frog, he needs to develop the disciplinary power of philosophy and education. The philosophy with a clear conception of its own nature must be a consistent form of a comparative discipline; otherwise, just as the various religious and educational systems of the world are beset with jealousy and antagonism, philosophy, too, suffers by the split into friendly and unfriendly forces. This is fundamentally an error generated by the ignorant retention of a false conception of self. In the present world of ideological conflict and confusion, it is an urgent matter to foster a truly comparative philosophy in the hope of transcending the deplorable straits man is in and work toward a profound peace that encompasses the whole run of mankind.

Philosophy as the foundation of all disciplines

To establish world peace, the basic requirement is for a vision that encompasses the whole wide world as displayed by the hilltop frog. On the other side of the spectrum, the frog in the well with ego-oriented narrow vision is a sure sign of the rise of turbulence and disorderly struggle. It should be noted, however, that the position of the hilltop frog is not gratuitous, for it would take the common man much education, dedication, and training to attain the level of intuitive synthetic judgment. Buddhism, in this respect, has taught the nature of emptiness (*śūnyatā*), the capture of the basis of supreme synthetic judgment, for the past 2500 years which was started by the historical Buddha and continued by the patriarchs of Buddhist schools. Compared with this, the Greek period early on started the dichotomous existence of man in terms of the *intellectus* and *ratio* and the dual function of synthetic and analytic judgments. Although the *intellectus* was assigned to the realm of God in Christianity, it need not necessarily be so, since, by God, the intuitive synthetic judgment can be transformed from the unconscious to the conscious realm. This quickly reminds us of St. Paul's immortal words, "I live no longer alone; Christ lives through me." With such religious faith in God displayed in the West, Kant, too, need not have stopped with analytic judgment but could have penetrated the realm of intuitive synthetic judgment. Put another way, to coax the frog in the well to get out and mount the hill for a commanding overview ought to be the principle of all religions, the fundamental element of the educational process, and the basis for the shift from combative to peaceful order in society. Thus, it can be concluded that the teachings in East-West religions are fundamentally the same and so is the process of opening up of man's mind. No other means of livelihood exists for man but to live his life to the fullest extent.

What is man?

"What is philosophy?" was answered by the Greeks as "know thyself." This same answer is applicable to the question, "What is man?" Thus, in considering the question of the universe, the Greek period exhibited a remarkable talent for focussing on man's capacity to view things and to enter the depths of his psychological makeup which resulted in the division of the *intellectus* and *ratio*.

As it is extremely difficult to lead someone to become conscious of the nature of the *intellectus* in the educational process, it becomes a very important focus, as well as an arduous task. If the realization of this frame of mind is to become the point of departure in education, then there is the grave danger that the synthetic judgment will be closed off suddenly by the elements of the intuitive unconscious, the status of ordinary perception. This being the case, it would require the wise or tough disciplinarian to exert tremendous effort to realize the *intellectus*. However difficult the task may be, it cannot be avoided if it focuses on the crisis or turning point in the transformation of consciousness from the nonenlightened to enlightened realm of existence. We could certainly imagine how painful it must have been for the sages of old to press this point home.

This focal point corresponds analogously to the discovery of the zero in mathematics, the birth of God in religion, and the emptiness or mutual penetration of being and nonbeing in the realm of reason, as taught in Buddhism, all of which are so difficult to delineate. Even language falls far short of adequate expression. Yet it is astounding to know now that Greek philosophy had philosophized from true man's perspective and attained a proper epistemological stance to probe the fringes of the theory of mind's structure.

The next major contribution in the West is by the Christian church fathers. The matter of judgment in the afterlife aside, they assiduously studied Greek philosophy and discovered the authentic source of preserving Christianity by relating the birth of God to the focal point of the unconscious, i.e., the possibility of intuitive synthetic judgment in man. This affirms the great insight and profoundness of the church fathers.

In the East, the Buddha was the first in recorded history to give focus on the completion of personality (attainment of Buddhahood) based on the realization of the mind-base. Throughout Buddhist history and development, this realization became the core, especially as seen in the various texts of the Mahāyāna tradition, and also became the basis for education because it provided an explanation that could reach the masses.

As the nature of the mind is the same for all, if its true realization in terms of the mind-base as characterized by nonorigination and nonextinction were accomplished, needless struggles of the two frogs in the well could be avoided, and all efforts could be directed toward the accomplishment of a peaceful, lofty, true man. The accomplishment would affirm the cogency of the Buddhist doctrine that all men could attain Buddhahood, i.e., all beings are, without exception, endowed with Buddha-nature and could activate it. This is the realm of *satori*, the actualization of *prajñā*-emptiness in the Mahāyāna, depicting the diagram of the mind-base founded on the emptiness of the five aggregates of being. The diagram became the doctrine of One Mind in the *Awakening of Faith in the Mahāyāna*, and the doctrine in an expanded form expounds on the principle of realizing true manhood.

Needless to say, other Buddhist texts give exhaustive analyses of the process involved in the movement from the ignorant to enlightened realms of existence.

We would be hard put to seek elsewhere for something, besides the realization of the mind-base, that constitutes the fundamental principle of the educational process, basis of learning, and the authentic grounds of existence. Even in considering the phenomena of the Axial Age (fifth–sixth century B.C.) in which we have witnessed the great cultural flourishes in Europe, India, and China, focussing on the central issues concerning God, man, and the world (society), we are able to discern and confirm the function of the universally given structure of the mind. It would be a confirmation of the Buddhist doctrine of One Mind, Two Aspects and Three Perspectives that each mind manifests in intimating with the truth of existence.

Christianity is said to be monotheistic and Buddhism polytheistic or even pantheistic. But it should be noted that Christianity has the doctrine of the Trinity, i.e., Godhead manifested as Father, Son, and the Holy Spirit; Buddhism has its Three Treasures, i.e., Buddha, Dharma, and Sangha or the doctrine of Three Bodies (*trikāya*), i.e., The Body of Dharma, The Body of Transformation, and The Body of Bliss. The doctrines of both religions, I believe, suggest a close kinship between the realization of the mind-base and the actual social educational process, i.e., that learning starts with the proper focus on the structure of the mind which transcends mere logicality in order to open up the total realm of existence. Education, in this respect, is an ever-widening experience, as everyone would attest.

I would now like to expand on the educational process by applying what we have been discussing so far to the present Japanese educational system. In order to examine the principles used in the present system, I have previously made an investigation by applying the method of psychological structuralism to the present Japanese Constitution, especially in reference to Article 1, "The Aims of Education," of the Basic Education Law.[11] The reason for this investigation is that, although the ancient sages of Greece, Christian world, and India paid strict attention to the area of man's education and psychological structures (realm of epistemology), contemporary Western philosophy generally lacks any complete analysis of the mind, and it may not be in error to assert that epistemology has left the central scene of philosophy. The result has been, unfortunately, to continue to nourish or educate human beings by being restricted to the ordinary, common sense, logistic 'frog in the well' method. Though new forms of 'structuralism' have appeared in the West of late, they are still far short of what we have been discussing as psychological structuralism (qua epistemology).

Despite all the shortcomings, however, we earnestly hope for the day to come soon when Eastern and Western philosophies will be able to move ahead united in the same direction. While savoring this hope, I wish to declare that an identical psychological structure resides in the Eastern, as well as the Western, mind.

It goes without saying that the four principles of the Japanese Constitution are pacifism, democracy, cultural nation, and welfare state. Relating these principles to the concepts found in the *Awakening of Faith in the Mahāyāna* and the *Mahāparinirvāṇa Sūtra*, the following correspondences are drawn.

Japanese Constitution	*Awakening of Faith in the Mahāyāna*	*Mahāparinirvāṇa Sūtra*
	(enlightened nature)	(features of nirvāṇa)
1. pacifism	permanence	permanence
2. democracy	unchanging	true self
3. cultural nation	pure Dharma (*satori*)	enjoyment, bliss
4. welfare state	permanent abode	purity (pure realm)

When the above is adapted to the diagram of psychological structuralism, the following diagram results.

culture (God, truth)

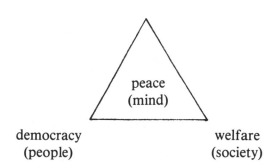

democracy   welfare
(people)   (society)

Article 1, Aims of Education, projects:

1. fulfillment of character building
2. formation of a peaceful nation and society
3. embrace truth and righteousness
4. value individual's worth
5. respect
6. maintain responsibility
7. aspire independent spirit

8. nourish a healthy mind
9. nourish a healthy body
10. aspire wholesome citizenry.

The correspondence of the above ten points with the diagram of the mind-base results in the following diagrams.

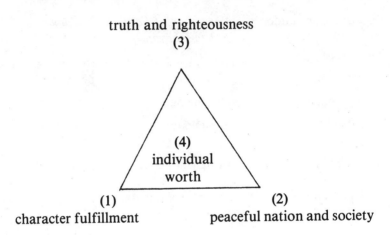

truth and righteousness
(3)

(4)
individual
worth

(1)
character fulfillment

(2)
peaceful nation and society

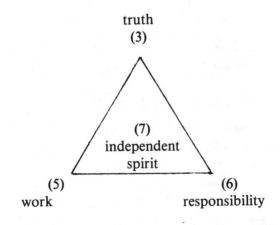

truth
(3)

(7)
independent
spirit

(5)
work

(6)
responsibility

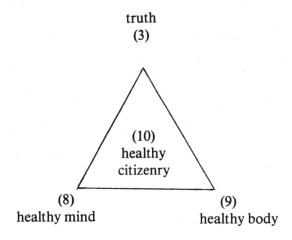

truth
(3)

(10)
healthy
citizenry

(8)
healthy mind

(9)
healthy body

The diagrams show the congruence of elements with the Western metaphysical scheme, as, for example, in the triadic relationship of God, man (people), and the world (society). They also corroborate and affirm Eastern thought enunciated previously in the doctrine from the *Kegon* (*Hua-yen*) *Sūtra*: "Three realms are merely one mind; No separate Dharma outside the mind; The mind, Buddha, and sentient creatures are not differentiated."

When the Constitution of Japan and the Basic Education Law are considered together, they conform to the Four Virtues of Nirvāṇa (permanence, true self, enjoyment, purity) and the Four Vows to save all sentient beings uttered by the Buddha and later by his incarnate, the Bodhisattva Dharmākara. The Constitution, interestingly enough, is often said to have been forced upon the Japanese while, on the other hand, the Education Law had been written by a committee which included many Japanese members. But what is surprising is that these documents seem to have been written based on Buddhist principles. Why the resemblance? My thoughts are that they reflect and confirm the presence and function of the realization of the mind-base.

In the present educational scene, the following situation has come to pass. Lectures on freedom and democracy go on all the time. The question is, however, how much understanding of the spirit of the democratic constitution and the basic education law do these lecturers have? I am afraid the answer is, very little.

Examining matters within the same context of democracy, there seems to be some vast difference in the Soviet democratic constitution promulgated after World War I and the present Japanese Constitution. On the other hand, we must ask ourselves if philosophers should be swayed by the presence of diverse camps or ideologies in comparative thought, such as, the right or the left, and the old or the new? If that should ever happen at all, not only comparative thought but the very substance of philosophy would be in grave jeopardy. In weighing the present situation, it would be fruitful, I believe, for comparative studies to take the initial step by utilizing psychological diagrams derived from the profound insights and principles relative to being that already exist in the classical texts of both the East and West. It must be said, finally, that the real purpose of comparative philosophy must not be mere academic ideological studies but must move forward to bring forth real dialogic substance based on a unified method and goal.

Chapter II

The Logic of Unity

— Discovery of zero and emptiness in prajñāpāramitā *thought —*

The Reason for a Logic of Unity

I wish to present the logic of unity in a condensed and simplified form supported by ten articles that concurrently elucidate the fundamental principles of Buddhism. Without the elucidation, there would be no clear conception of the Buddhist thrust to any intended East-West dialogue. Moreover, I will discuss the articles within the context of the fundamental mode of thinking.

The terms East and West are not very clear geographical and cultural concepts, but, since they are frequently and customarily used, I will retain their usage. On another note, the shadow of religion casts deeply in the recesses of many ideas. The two religions that have had the greatest impact in the present world are, needless to say, Christianity (which includes Judaism) and Buddhism, representing the West and East, respectively. But rather than geographic concepts, it may be better to refer to them as maps reflecting different modes of thinking, as applied in Japan, for example, in reference to the possibility of setting up a dialogue that involves Eastern and Western wisdom. This is certainly not the time to clearly demarcate friend and foe or Eastern and Western blocks but, more importantly, a time for each and everyone to rid oneself of the narrow self-imposed perspective and initiate a dialogue within the larger context that includes both East and West.

Sociology, for example, must ideally take up the discipline of the science of man and proceed in accordance with the advances made in the various special fields of endeavor in general without losing its integrative power. As it presently does not seem to have hold of this power, it is most compelling that it set out to discover a new direction by removing the restrictive ideological shell it is in and engage in an open dialogue encompassing Eastern and Western views.

Metaphysical Bias and True Human Orientation

In examining the differnt modes of thinking in the East and West, generally speaking, it can be said that the West maintains a strong metaphysical bias. This has been the case traditionally where there is a premising of an original source of being, such as God or Nature, from which man and the rest of the creation follow. In simple terms, the Western mode of thinking based heavily on Christianity is as follows:

God created man in his own image. (creation theory)
Man, in turn, creates a society patterned after his own image.
(principle of reaping the fruit of one's own labor)

Between the two expressions, there is only a slight difference in the format, but as modes of thinking the end results spell out great differences. If God were postulated first and the rest of creation came later, then it would only be natural that man should conform with the laws of nature or with divine providence. And should freedom be granted to man, his actions would be limited to whether or not he believes in God's omnipotence or whether or not he is aware of his own sins. It simply would be too farfetched to think that one could determine one's own action or change the course of history. This is related to the problem of historical necessity or freedom. As such a way of thinking still lingers in the background of Western thought, it forces us to seriously consider relinquishing the metaphysical framework in the mode of thinking and to take up the true human orientation as the basis of thinking.

In this connection, let us consider the Marx-Engels view of man and the world which is taken to be a most progressive and

representative view today. Although Engels contributed enor-
mously in developing Marxian philosophy, on his own he
presented a modern definition of materialism and idealism. He
states thus:[1]

> The great basic question of all philosophy, especially of modern
> philosophy, is that concerning the relation of thinking and being.
> . . . .the question: which is primary, spirit or nature—that ques-
> tion, in relation to the Church, was sharpened into this: "Did god
> create the world or has the world been in existence eternally?" The
> answer which the philosophers gave to this question split them into
> two great camps. Those who asserted the primacy of spirit to
> nature, and, therefore, in the last instance, assumed world creation
> in some form or other—(and among the philosophers, Hegel, for
> example, this creation often becomes still more intricate and im-
> possible than in Christianity)—comprised the camp of idealism.
> The others, who regarded nature as primary, belong to the various
> schools of materialism.

There are two undeniable facts that can be drawn from the
above quote. The first is that both materialism and idealism are
bound to a metaphysical mode of thinking. The question of God's
creation of the world is in the Old Testament. Whether the source
of being is spirit or nature, the overriding conception of existence
still maintains its same unchangeable character. Each is a
metaphysical monism, and both are considered to be the same, in-
sofar as the mode of thinking is concerned, just as the palms of the
right and left hands are entirely different but both resemble each
other very much. It would seem ridiculous, therefore, to have both
compete with each other for their respective supremacy. The real
problem here is that the principle of the source of being will
regulate everything and thereby inevitably rupture and alienate
man from the truth of existence.

The second fact is that Engels wrote the work about a hundred
years ago, in 1888 to be exact, which reveals in a surprising way
that metaphysics had become the central issue of philosophic problems and that a clear cleavage between idealism and materialsim
was already in evidence.

The question of metaphysics, curiously enough, was taken up by
Kant way before Engels, but Kant denied its place and function.

Kant, however, attempted to philosophize from the standpoint of pure reason because the problem of the source of the universe transcended time and space, which concepts constituted for him the only means of exhibiting thought process. Accordingly, philosophy is unable to successfully answer metaphysical questions. It is interesting to note here that the historical Buddha more than 2500 years ago resolved the question of metaphysics on the same Kantian grounds, i.e, indeterminable nature. Prior to the Buddha, in India, the same metaphysical questions were debated with variant answers given, for example, on the nature of the supreme being. There is a Buddhist text[2] which describes how one Mālunkyaputta kept raising metaphysical questions and threatened to leave the monkhood if the Buddha did not explain those questions plausibly. There was complete philosophical justification for the Buddha to deny the raising of such questions. It is therefore a surprising phenomenon to see such questions posed only about a hundred years ago in Western philosophy and such attitudes still being continued today in progressive, scientific, and educational quarters.

Since Marx and Engels were not considered to be mainline philosophers, it would not be strictly necessary to introduce them in the educational field. Were they ever to be considered in the field, it would be a grave error to classify them in the progressive, modern, scientific circles. There may be some who cast doubt on our sincerity, saying that we are out to slander or demean Marxism. There are some in Japan, on the other hand, who treat Marxist thought as being very scientific and progressive. If, however, the scientific attitude were to be taken, one would have to approach things with complete rationality. I am neither an adherent nor a detractor of Marxism. The problem here is not what party one affiliates with in politics or what ideology one upholds; it is one of viewing things with absolute objectivity.

Education must be very strict but fair. To permit freedom of speech or ideology means that there is a trust in man's basic intelligence and a liberality in the educational process. It would be totally disastrous were education swayed by power struggles or by profit and loss motives, for the freedom of education in the deepest sense is intimately tied up with the truth of existence.

From the impartial standpoint, Marxism, in the words of Engels, has a metaphysical and religious foundation and, in particular, a strong Judaic influence. Judging it objectively now, it cannot be considered to manifest the spirit of science and rationality, although allowance must be made with respect to the difference between the Marxist movement and Marxist thought. This is quite similar to the situation in Buddhism where there is a difference between the Buddhist movement and Buddhist thought.

In listing the corresponding points between Marxism and Judaism, we note certain special characteristics, such as, a strong sense of a folk religion, the lack of universal nature of love, and the indistinguishable nature of the realms of religion and government.

	Judaism	Marxism
1.	strong religious belief	fanatical and extremely combative attitude toward opposing ideas which prevents matters from being settled peacefully
2.	monotheism based on a supreme, absolute God and denial of alien beliefs	materialism
3.	rule by laws which are God's commandments	dialectical method
4.	historical fate which is deterministic and prophetic	historical materialism
5.	chosen people	class consciousness
6.	eschatology	autonomy of the worker
7.	establish the Kingdom of God	nonexploited communist society (classless society)

The above correspondences were made not to attack or deny Marxism, as such, but because the nonrational points mentioned become objects of analysis for those of us who aim at a purely scientific orientation. Granting the existence of religious and ideological freedom, still, the basic or supreme freedom must lie in the freedom of the educational process itself, since the implementation of it is the mission of higher education.

The Limits of Religion and the Social Sciences

As will be explained later, both religion and the social sciences essentially must have certain limitations. Being free from government control, religion must not meddle with government or economic activities. Unchecked use of freedom, however, cannot be true freedom. But it can be said that the nature of true freedom is the most basic subject matter in the social sciences. Accordingly, there must be a respect for a clear, mutually limiting realm of activity in religion and the social sciences. Whether it concerns a religion or an individual or group, freedom that is one-sided and unchecked cannot be considered to be true freedom in any society.

Now, it may be possible to establish metaphysical truths by faith alone. But were this faith extended into the realm of the social sciences, it would raise havoc and be analogous to denying the devotee his religious freedom, i.e., a simple case of a violation in reverse order. The basis of freedom in the social sciences is based on rational dialogues on truths relative to all human beings. This means that from the standpoint of the sciences there is always a return to rationality and humanity.

In religion, without faith in the absolute nature of God, faith itself could not be established. This amounts to the commitment of self-contradiction since faith is required in order to establish itself. A hidden problem exists whereby the solution is blocked if the total human awareness, including religious consciousness, is not established. This is probably the major reason why there are voices heard calling attention to the impasse reached in Western civilization. In such a situation, it is no wonder that there is an increasing number of Western scholars who are turning to the study of Buddhism. Buddhist books may be very popular, but in Japan it is regretful that there are only a few scholars interested in Buddhism in a serious way.

Progress in education is not accomplished by a one-sided dedication to a cause but, rather, by constant questioning and critique of the issues. It is important, of course, to have faith and dedication in one's own theory, but it is even more important at the same time to listen to opposing views. Consequently, it is most urgent that a nonmetaphysical nature of Buddhism become an object of research in the field of social sciences which had long been dominated and nourished by the false notion of supremacy of Western philosophy and methodology. The incorporation of Buddhism in such research may well be Japan's unique way of contributing to world thought. Buddhism is not merely found in the dust-ridden classical texts but should be brought out in the shining light of the world scene by its incorporation in the social scientific studies. I cannot emphasize with too much the urgency that Buddhist truths must not be left buried in neglected texts.

The Nature of Buddhism

Since Buddhism is antimetaphysical, its greatest asset is in its truly rational nature centered on man himself. Today, as we take note of the collapse of the Western metaphysical image of man, Buddhism, which did not expect this new mission to be enthrusted upon her, naturally must now make its appearance on the novel contemporary social scene. Unfortunately, there is a great obstacle. That is to say, due to its 2500 years of spread and development, it has evolved into a bulky and unwieldy mass such that it is extremely difficult, though not impossible, to bring into manageable focus in social science research, since no common ground of discourse is readily found. Buddhism today is simply too varied and extended compared to its original form. The difficulties keep mounting, but, in the field of social sciences which serves as a general principle of education, comparatively speaking, it would not be too difficult to focus on the issues and understand matters. To overcome the difficulties and to associate the issues in the context of the social sciences would naturally be limited to an extremely few people.

It is a fact that today Buddhism is explained with all the variety of forms and attendant complexities. Left in this situation, it would most likely start and end as just another commonplace way of life. Its most original thought as condensed in the so-called doctrine of equality qua differentiation (*byōdō soku sabetsu*),[3] a most penetrative academic cutting edge, would slip away unnoticed and remain in oblivion. Also, in the various social sciences, such as, law, economics, political science, humanities, and so forth, which cover many fields and facets of life, it would be extremely difficult to find a common thread that runs through them to achieve a unifying science of man. The result would be mere accumulation of a vast variety of information or merely describing human nature or a being that is impotent in relating to individual concrete practical matters.

As Buddhism has a history of development as a religion, the doctrine of equality qua differentiation and, vice versa, differentiation qua equality will not be understood properly, owing to the fact that the emphasis will be predominantly on the nature of equality with an extremely weak emphasis on differentiation.

In the sciences, however, while keeping in mind the nature of equality, the task will be necessitated by explaining the nature of differentiation by involving Buddhism as a social science. In so doing, the real meaning of the doctrine will be realized. But it will not be realized under the present complex situation in which Buddhism continues.

So I have decided right now to abandon Buddhism completely. Why? Because to utter "Buddhism! Buddhism!," is actually to vitiate and deviate from Buddhism itself. What is needed in Buddhism today is the right posture or stance toward social life without being overwhelmed by the texts or expressions. The real text that we should all be reading right now is the reality of society right before our eyes. In reading it as it is, we will give birth to a proper science of society, for the people in society are the most important, followed by those who read the reality of society.

Thinking thus, I decided to learn about that stance or posture from Buddhism. This is not difficult at all, since it consists merely in accepting the dictum that "truth remains the only truth." It should be noted that man is endowed a priori with the power to distinguish what is truth and what is not. This is the only basic attitude required for those of us who are engaged in Buddhist social scientific studies.

To expand on the matter, to assert "truth is truth" means in Buddhism that "man is endowed with the Buddha-nature." Both assertions truly express the Buddhist fundamental attitude as confirmed by the Buddha's final words recorded in the *Mahāparinirvāṇa Sūtra.*[4]

Be ye lamps unto yourselves;
Do not rely on others.
Uphold the law (Dharma) as the lamp;
Do not uphold any other.

Consequently, the problem of attitude or stance is a most important teaching of Buddhism, but it is actually a means of learning about one's own personality and not merely restricted to intellectual exercise. It is also closely related to the Four Marks of non-self, impermanence, nirvāṇa, and suffering—indeed, the assertion "truth is truth" may be taken to refer to each of the Marks. Should we then accommodate the truth that all is suffering, then all problems of life in the world would be treated as a science of man in the realm of the social sciences. In this respect, the social sciences would not be specialized sciences but would rightly be an integrative science where the problem of attitude will be addressed in man's social life. All is suffering means, first of all, to negate everything, i.e., the negation of the truth of existence (Dharma).

With respect to the other Marks, we may expand as follows. The concept of nirvāṇa means that there is emptiness as well as peace and tranquility. It also means that at the point of transcendence of the negation of everything there will be the solution to all problems. The concept of impermanence refers to the fact that all actions are impermanent. The concept of non-self, finally, refers to the nonsubstantiality of all *dharmas*, the factors of experience. The Four Marks can be discussed endlessly on the intellectual level. Essentially, truth is the only truth, and there is no truth that can be delineated by metaphysics.

The above analysis reveals my attitude or stance that I take. In it, I have established the attitude to be taken in social science research, as well as the so-called social text to be read. The text refers to the facts that occur daily in society, but, if we do not have a language, there is no way the text could be read at all.

In Christianity, interestingly enough, the Bible says: "In the beginning was the Word and the Word was God." Reflecting on the matter, could we not say that language was probably the very first element in man? As we have language, immediately, we are able to discover the source of religion and the beginning of the Buddhist Dharma.

In the past, man had used a variety of logic. Since errors exist in language itself, it was difficult to transmit truth from one person to another or from one mind to another. So, we must be very careful and think thoroughly on what can be utilized in that particular logic (language).

I have given much thought to mankind's discovery up to now in regard to the question, "What is the highest form of logic achieved?" Judging on the basis of tangible evidences, I have arrived at a very simple conclusion which is nothing but the familiar mathematical equation: $1 + 2 = 3$. As this simple logic is readily acceptable by all, I have used it as a starting point to raise the questions, for example, "What is the integer 1?" or "What is an equation?" By thus questioning, I have been able to seek out the proper foundation for the mode of thinking of man. In consequence, I offer the following ten articles on the Logic of Unity which expound the nature of the mode of thinking. I will later examine them in detail.

Ten Articles on the Logic of Unity

1. The mutual entrance and penetration of characteristics (elements) (*sōsoku-sōnyū*) is similar in nature to mathematical infinite natural numbers where each member, without losing its self-nature (identity), constitute a unified totality. This phenomenon is also expressed by the concept of 'one-is-all' (*ichi-soku-issai*). It is man's perogative to realize his own total principle of being as expressed by this phenomenon.

2. Any arithmetic function (addition, subtraction, multiplication, division) that involves more than two natural numbers will always produce a single result whereby the parts and the whole interpenetrate (mutually ingress). In consequence, the equation is the basic form of the dialectic.

3. Since the whole being is dialectical in nature, the whole concept is in the nature of being (i.e., 'is') as well as singular (i.e., 'it'). The principle and the actual fact

(event) interpenetrate to give rise to proper understanding.

4. The zero and the infinite are in a relationship of contradictory self-unity or antinomical self-identity (*mujunteki-jiko-dōitsu*), and this phenomenon is otherwise called emptiness (*śūnyatā*). And on account of emptiness everything will come into being, and, at the same time, paradoxically, everything will be prevented from coming into being.

5. Emptiness and life itself (value) are beyond conception. They are open secrets, as it were, belonging to the realm of faith; to discuss them is to complicate and trivialize matters, but then, without understanding them in terms of the total nature of being, nothing will arise.

6. All concepts have the two realms of being and emptiness. That is why the conventional and absolute nature of things (i.e., dual truths) interpenetrate.

7. In a singular vision or eye-consciousness, there will necessarily appear a singular eye-realm. There should be no transcendental or extraneous imposition and construction.

8. Body, speech, and will are basically a singular act where they all mutually interpenetrate. Therefore, work or activity is not a simple matter of time.

9. The open mind allows complete interpenetration of elements to mold a free personality, but when it is closed it transforms itself into the nature of ignorance and delusion which become the basis of universal suffering.

10. Dialectic has the meaning of separate function yet ultimately a unified nature relative to personality, truth, and righteousness and becomes the basis of a correct view of life and the world.

Preliminary to the discussion of the above in more detail, I would like to present the following doctrines, known as the Kegon

(Hua-yen) Ten Profound Gates, which depict in very subtle ways the way experiential reality exists.[5]

The Kegon Ten Profound Gates

1. The simultaneous correspondence and completion of events. Or, the phenomena of events in instant mutuality in terms of time and space.

2. The free and nonobstructive nature of events in their character of intension and extension. Or, the phenomena of events in instant mutuality in terms of intension and extension.

3. The mutual penetration of the one and the many natures of events without the loss of identities. Or, the phenomena of events in instant mutuality in terms of singularity and plurality or the one and all (many).

4. The freedom and instant mutuality of the various *dharmas* (i.e., experiential factors). Or, the phenomena of events in instant mutuality in terms of beings in space.

5. The complementariness of the manifest and unmanifest natures of events. Or, the phenomena of events in instant mutuality in terms of what are seen and unseen.

6. The accommodation of the one in the many and the many in the one. Or, the phenomena of events in instant mutuality in terms of greatness and smallness.

7. The realm of existence as depicted by the metaphor of Indra's Net (i.e., the limitless mutual reflection or penetration of all events). Or, the phenomena of events in instant mutuality and mutual penetration.

8. The unpretentious clear manifestation of events. Or, the phenomena of events in instant mutuality in terms of objective fact and principle.

9. The establishment of mutual penetration of events in the ten periods of time (i.e., the three temporal moments

mutually penetrate each other to produce nine periods and the nine periods together comprise a single moment, thus the ten periods). Or, the phenomena of events in instant mutuality in terms of their inner and outer temporal natures (i.e., so-called horizontal and vertical temporal dimensions).

10. The completion of perfect harmony and illumination between the chief and underling i.e., the subject and its object). Or, the phenomena of events in instant mutuality in terms of the subjective and objective realms.

The above comprise the principles of existence found in the *Kegon Sūtra*. Although I have added to each gate an explanation by way of the phenomena of events, they delineate essentially a dialectical structure and function based on the free character of events in time and space, beings in space, intension and extension, one and many, and manifest and unmanifest. By focussing on these principles that depict the truth of existence, it is possible to establish man's nature of freedom. We shall now proceed to discuss in detail the ten articles on the logic of unity.

Article 1

It is only in man that a special power exists whereby he has a holistic consciousness of the principles involved in which the infinite natural numbers do not lose their individual identities while allowing for a conception of a unified totality. This power is obviously the capture of the Buddhist doctrine of interrelational origination but expressed in terms of the axioms of natural numbers in mathematics. It is only proper that such be the case and that it constitutes the general thesis, as well as the conclusion or summation of the ten articles that are now being discussed. As a matter of fact, I believe that the various Buddhist doctrines are essentially reduced to this holistic nature of consciousness.

The age of the Buddha naturally did not show any development of dialectic or mathematics as we know them today. Such being the case, we can understand all the more the difficulty with which the teachings had to be expressed.

Although existing in the bulky *Kegon Sūtra*, the Ten Profound Gates can, for example, be explained in a condensed form of a mathematical principle. This is the tenor of the first article.

When the tenets of Kegon thought were allegedly first propounded by the Buddha to his ten top disciples, it is recorded that they were dumbfounded and muted. Clearly, without the aid of modern mathematics and dialectic, the situation would not improve. Now, fortunately, with the use of simple arithmetic principles, we are able to discern those tenets, i.e., an understanding by reference to basic principles inherent to the natural sciences, and relate them to the manner in which the human mind functions.

It would be naive and grossly insufficient to conclude, as many do, that the doctrine of interrelational origination is merely an ancient Buddhist way of thinking. We must rather be open enough to acknowledge the fact that the doctrine is a great discovery which exhibits the dynamic mutuality and interrelationality of all things and that it coincides beautifully with modern mathematical principles. It can further be argued that computers and moon travel have been made possible by utilizing these principles.

The doctrine, then, is not only a great discovery made some 2500 years ago, but it makes a great impact on the contemporary scene. It short, though separated by a great expanse of time, the idea inherent to the doctrine rings a contemporary note. The Buddha's times can be likened to the present age in that profound metaphysical ways of thinking were rampant in an ambience of free thought but an age nevertheless constituted of ideological confusion. In other words, the Buddha's age was characterized by contentious movements, such as, nihilism, skepticism, and materialism, many of which are familiar to us today. It constitutes a great insight to rise above the merely metaphysical nature of the doctrine and to perceive its structure in the very nature of man's own being. What is more, its principle now can be readily seen and aptly applied to the realm of the social and physical sciences.

It is told that the Buddha himself was highly skeptical about transmitting the doctrine to the masses because of its inherent profundity and had even thought of enjoying all to himself the nature of the enlightened state of existence. Fortunately for us today, we are able to comprehend the form of its nature readily due to the advances in mathematics and dialectical process. Unfortunately, however, there are still many today who regard the truth discussed in philosophy and the social sciences to be entirely different from the one in the natural sciences. On the other hand, there are scholars who would not hesitate to openly profess the wholly relative nature of all truths and dash any hopes of aiming at a singular truth of existence.

Is it not the case, however, that because truth has been returned to man himself the modern era swiftly opened up and restored freedom to man? Were truth relative and plural, it would cease to be truth at all; on the other hand were all principles united in the total consciousness of a person, truth would become a major focus of education. However narrow and specialized the subdivisions of field of research, there would always be the total nature of man's consciousness, as a man, which becomes the basis of learning. I believe it would be very dangerous for a person to engage in learning without this total consciousness; for, although learning is undoubtedly within man's enterprise, he would likely err in taking his own field to be the only truthful realm of activity.

The disgrace and downfall of a culture usually begin with the appearance of those individuals whose consciousness is narrow and limited. In Japan proper, instances of such narrowness can be seen in such movements as the overemphasis on and unbridled pride in securing with whatever means one's own individual home or the total lack of national spirit. This can be attributed, I believe, to the postwar Japanese educational system which was grossly deficient in instilling in students the total consciousness on the reality of things.

True realization by an individual could not arise without the simultaneous consciousness of the individual and total nature of things. The Japanese society, for instance, is presently in an age that relishes absolute freedom, but, unfortunately, it is in confusion. The youths are confused, and, while the universities are also in the state of confusion, the responsibility for education is shuffled about by blaming home training, politics, or society itself, all of which indicates that there is a lack of total human consciousness.

Total or holistic consciousness means the realization that everything is related to everything else by virtue of interrelational origination. To merely gloss over the question, "What is man?" with "A most difficult question indeed," or "What is freedom?" with "A novel question," would only bring about confusion on the part of the learner.

Man's gravest pitfall today is his lack of holistic consciousness and his quest for an independent absolute self which is nothing but an excessively distorted type of individualism. The roots of educational and social confusion can be found in the nonholistic consciousness of individuals such that, for example, a Christian may claim Christianity to represent all religions, a Buddhist may claim supremacy and absoluteness over other religions, and a nation may claim hegemony over other nations.

The fundamental aim of Buddhist teaching is to emphasize the significance of interrelational origination and to arouse in each person the sense of the holistic consciousness. It is also to stress that this consciousness should always be kept as the initial foundation of research in the social sciences. At the same time, since equality and discrimination are mutually penetrative concepts, it is necessary to clarify the differences that exist in the nature of the disciplines and their respective subject matters, i.e., between natural and social sciences, politics and economics, and religion and sociology.

In its long history, Buddhism has promulgated itself as a religion emphasizing the aspect of the equality of all beings. At the same time, it has denied discriminative knowledge as being deleterious and in error. But the true science of man is possible only by following the dictum, "equality is at once discrimination and discrimination is at once equality." Forgetting this dictum, no Buddhist-based social science research would ever materialize.

It can be said that holistic consciousness is also the fundamental principle of love. Only when one is able to be conscious of the totality of things in their oneness can there be love of fellow human beings, love of a nation, and even love of thy neighbor. At the same time, since Buddhist thought is in the nature of a dialectic, reason should be emphasized on the discriminative level, and the nature of discrimination itself ought to be refined or crystallized. So, by expounding on both realms of love and reason, Buddhist dialectic of experience would be realized.

In the following Article 2, we shall examine how dialectical thinking arises from the principles of natural mathematics and what status it will be provided by the dialectic. In Article 3, we shall examine how to apply the mathematical principles when they are expanded into a general concept to become the principles of logic in general. From Article 4 and on, we shall indicate the principles of dialectic applicable to the social sciences.

Article 2

Any function (i.e., addition, subtraction, multiplication, and division) of two or more natural numbers will necessarily produce a uniform result, and the parts and the whole will interpenetrate. In consequence, the equation is the basic form of the dialectic and enables the achievement of a proper cognition in terms of the interpenetration of objective facts and principle.

As dialectic has become a fundamental question in philosophy, as well as in the social sciences, this article faces that question and accommodates the problematics on such matters as why dialectic is related to truth and how that comes about.

In any philosophical inquiry of man, it is forbidden to think that since it is dialectical it must be the truth or that it is the truth merely because Hegel or Marx said it or because it is the cumulative integration of the most advanced theories of the 19th century. We must pause here to reflect on the Buddhist creed: "Reliance not on man but on the Dharma." It is a creed that is compellingly cogent to the philosophical study of man.

It was earlier mentioned that the truth is the truth, regardless of whether or not a famous person stated it so. One must, in short, become the very subject of the judgment. This is known as the self-embodiment of truth or self-illumination (*jitōmyō*). Would it ever be possible to convince everyone that Marxian dialectic expresses the truth relative to all phenomena in society? This is highly doubtful. Such a dialectic may perhaps be applicable to the realm where the law of the survival of the fittest finds meaning, but such a realm is also relative to the animal world and would deny the function of an educational process wherein the nature of man is in reference to his total consciousness. Such a dialectic, moreover, expresses a law that may be extended to certain parts of the underdeveloped world. But, so long as the image of man confronts the central question, "What is man?" it would be inapplicable and rendered null in any goals aspired in the training and education of a person.

I believe that it is necessary that man maintains an attitude that constantly quests for the truth. Furthermore, although it is said that there is no phenomenon called total consciousness, I do not believe that it is completely absent from the unconscious realm of man. The erroneous view stems from the present mode of teaching, which invariably results in such a view but which also exhibits the premature nature of the learning process. Despite this view, however, there is a vast storage of unique experiences by man from the past that we can fall back on and draw upon for inspiration. So that despite the temporary vagaries and shortcomings in perspectives and methods used by philosophy and the social sciences, the problem would not remain permanent, since man certainly exists with his many experiences. The disciplines, taken together, constitute the various paths to be taken, step by step, toward the realization of truth.

Since the consciousness of the whole person is the consciousness of man, it is not always to be set against the universe or mankind but should, instead, be considered in terms of particular questions relative to the free nature of man's intension and extension. In such a way, the basis of dialectic will be known in light of what is man's proper nature of thinking or what sort of principle of thinking is best suited for him.

In man's experiences so far, the logic that is accepted by all is that which functions in mathematics. The fact that man is in possession of this logic distinguishes him from other creatures that do not have it.

In considering what constitutes a proper logic, it is impossible to refer to a logic that ignores mathematical logic and that arises separately in the mind. It is only natural that mathematical logic is the model of a proper logic. Its basic structure is none other than the form found in a dialectic or a simple equation. It is possible to consider, paradoxically enough, that dialectic is the foundation of mathematical logic, as well as that which points at the basic form of a 'philosophical' logic. Strange as it may seem, up to now such positivistic truths as demonstrated in mathematical logic were not included in philosophical discourse. The principle of thinking that functions in both the natural sciences and philosophy is, after all, the same one that arises in all persons. Thus the basis of these disciplines are identical in this sense. Where can there be a difference?

There are today various forms of dialectic. Which one is the correct form? What is the nature of dialectic, anyway? How far may one use it? Can dialectic be used to foretell events in history? These are the kinds of questions that ought to be raised in the learning process; indeed, they constitute the very kernel of the study of man.

We may consider the basis of thinking in serial natural numbers thus: $\infty-1-1-1-1-0+1+1+1+1+\infty$. If this is the case, then whenever we answer in mathematical terms we are constantly in quest of the question, "What is the unit of an integer?" Incidentally, this idea lies at the bottom of why I have entitled my book The Logic of Unity (*Ichi-no-ronri*). When applied to philosophy, the question becomes, for example, "What is man?" "What is the nation?" "What is freedom?" — all of which are pointing at the unit or the relationship that exists between the one and the many. It is, moreover, identical to the process involved in algebra or the four basic arithmetic functions.

The rise of social scientific and experimental approach to things is based on clarifying such principles as the mutuality of the notions of equality (identity) and discrimination (difference). We must seriously reflect upon our own existence and not commit the error of the proverbial crab that falls into a hole to claim total view of the world, although it only has limited vision. Analogously, we must cease to make such doctrinal claims as dialectic alone is the principle of existence or that it is the principle of thinking by fixating on something at the expense of denying others.

Article 3

As all concepts (nouns as well as pronouns) have a dialectical nature, they constitute a unit ("it") and they also exist ("is"); moreover, they become proper cognitive elements by virtue of the phenomena of events (or factors of experience) in the state of instant mutuality of objective fact and principle.

Mathematics is considered to be the highest form of logic devised by man and has clearly evidenced itself today as the foundation for the development of the natural sciences. Even so, the further question becomes, "In what relationship is it to the generally known science of logic and philosophy?" This article will address that question.

When one thinks in terms of existence ("is"), it is already based on the fundamental principle of $a + b = c$ *or* $1 + 2 = 3$. In that case, as stated in Article 2, it already indicates the function of the principle of "instantaneity of universal and particular or one and many." This principle is not only relative to natural numbers but, as seen above, also transformable into algebraic equations. In the case of natural numbers, there is a uniform order in the mutuality of the numbers themselves which are taken to have existential nature, thus opening up the possibility of discovering certain mathematical principles present therein. In the case of algebraic equations which are transformable into other general concepts, the premise must be the orderly established factual relationship.

Herein lies the boundary between logic and mathematical principles. However, regarding the point that dialectic is based on man's original principle of thinking, there is no difference between the two. To demonstrate this fact, let us examine the basic form of ordinary language. In language, the form takes either the positive ("it is") or negative ("it is not") aspect. In the case of any noun or pronoun, the premise is primarily on its existent nature or on the unity or oneness (*ichi*). There is a constant reflection on something that exists, a coincidence of the principle of thinking and the principle of existence. Without this coincidence, it would be quite difficult to give the *raison d'etre* of all dialogues based on seemingly meaningless words. On the other hand, this is the way words carry such fundamental and universal meanings so as to be effectively used in the various languages.

From the above analysis, we should know what the nature of dialectic is, that it is based on the unique principle of thinking man. In addition, I firmly believe that the basis of philosophy and the social sciences can be found where there is a clear delineation of boundaries and discrimination of all matters based on the principle of "all is one and one is all." Accordingly, it should be recognized that our view of dialectic is vastly different from what the social sciences regard as metaphysical truths.

The fundamental principle is expressed in Buddhism in terms of the famous Eightfold Noble Path.[6] When confronted with this Noble Path, the Western mind usually raises the question, "What is the 'right'?" or "How could one know the 'right' without first knowing the 'wrong'?" In Buddhism, however, the fundamental principle of thinking is based on a unique dialectical nature, i.e., the principle of interrelational origination (*innen* or *engi, pratītya-samutpāda*). From it, then, it is possible to promote proper learning and to apply it to the whole spectrum of the social sciences.

When the Eightfold Noble Path is applied to the social sciences, its principle, as stated above, governs man's thinking process and can be related to modern disciplines roughly in the following manner.

Right view . . . . proper epistemology ⎤
Right thought . . . . proper conception ⎥
Right speech . . . . proper logic ⎥— philosophy
    (word) ⎥
Right action . . . . proper practical activity ⎦

Right livelihood . . . . proper view on life ⎤
Right energy . . . . proper effort ⎥— religion
Right mindfulness . . . . . proper social consciousness ⎥
Right meditation . . . . . . proper unity of mind ⎥
    (holistic consciousness) ⎦

The above scheme depicts the essential subject matters of the science of man. It focusses on a very important condition, i.e., the aims of the social sciences in which there is a unifying force in man to return everything to the unity of things. There are in Buddhism, for example, numerous lists of numbered doctrines (*hossū-myō-moku*). The Eightfold Noble Path is one of them. But the fact that all the other numbered doctrines come together to express the singular Buddhist Dharma signifies that there is a kind of dialectical logic involved in all, singularly as well as totally.

Article 4

It has already been asserted that the zero and infinite are in a relationship of contradictory self-unity (or antinomical self-identity), and this phenomenon has been referred to as emptiness (*kū; śūnyatā*). It should be noted further that emptiness expresses an epistemic position and has nothing to do with an existent matter. In consequence, in all experiences everything arises due to emptiness, and, conversely, without emptiness nothing arises.

Although the previous article dealt with mathematics as a model to relate to the inherent principle in the Buddhist doctrine of inter-relational origination, it also demonstrated the identity of the philosophical principle with that of the natural sciences and further cautioned that metaphysical principles are not applicable to these disciplines. In addition, it affirmed that Buddhism is always human-oriented and that the principle involved in interrelational origination is a basic dialectical form which penetrates all of the natural and social sciences.

From this article on we shall present the fundamental rule with which the mathematical principle could relate to the humanistic sciences (i.e., Buddhism), a rule that is capable of coping with all the questions in the social sciences by means of at least these seven remaining articles. We must therefore strive to affirm this fundamental rule, promote the social sciences widely, enrich them, and fulfill the development of the individual self. This is, after all, the teaching of self-enlightenment by the illumination of the Dharma. Indeed, it is the teaching of the historical Buddha as previously cited: "Be ye lamps unto yourselves. Do not rely on others. Let the Dharma be the lamp. Do not rely on anything else."

Not only do these words comprise a fundamental teaching but they are so relevant to us today that they ought to be the guideline for the establishment of the basic perspective of the learning process in the social sciences.

It should be noted here that, in terms of the highest meaning, the Buddhist concepts of man, truth, and freedom express the same reality of things. But this is not the case from the standpoint of ordinary meaning (i.e., conventional truth, *saṃvṛti-sat*). Transformed into an equation, the following would be the case:

truth + freedom = man
truth + freedom − man = 0

In observing the confused state of philosophy and social sciences, causes can be attributed to the confusion in the very fundamental question of what the social sciences stand for. More specifically, on the metaphysical level, the above three concepts could never come together, and this situation has generated a lot of confusion in the social sciences.

The discussion hardly seems to end. Let us bring things back into perspective by saying that this article will expand on the two concepts of zero and infinity in mathematics as akin to the Buddhist conception of contradictory self-unity (or antinomical self-identity) which are further expressed by the unique terms, emptiness (*kū*) and nonbeing (*mu*). Western philosophy, I believe, does not have this conception.

The fundamental features of Buddhism as depicted by the concepts of suffering, impermanence, and non-self all have as their basis the nature of emptiness. Although the concepts of emptiness and non-self are found everywhere in the texts, it should not cause one to turn away from Buddhism in dejection. On the other hand, we witness, for example, an entirely different perspective and understanding in mathematics. The history of mathematics clearly shows that the discovery of zero stimulated the phenomenal development in the modern period and that, without this discovery, the necessity of such concepts as infinity would never have arisen. It should be noted also that as logic in general maintains the same principle as mathematics, it becomes increasingly clear that correct judgment would not be possible without the concept of emptiness (i.e., the use of mathematical zero and infinity).

In Western philosophy, generally speaking, there are frequent references to the 'discovery of the self' or 'affirmation of the self.' But what good are these assertions if the concept of the 'self' is not clarified at the outset?

Some will surely criticize Buddhism for teaching the total annihilation of the self, rather than maintaining the ordinary concept of the self. This view is quite prevalent, but it ought to be corrected because the Buddhist concept of non-self uniquely delineates the nature of man understood from the standpoint of emptiness. In mathematical terms, it is analogous to man's nature after the discovery of the zero, as distinguished from the nature prior to the discovery. Thus, in Buddhism there is no 'self' blown out of existence but, rather, an understanding of a non-self phenomenon based on the total (holistic) consciousness of man. This should be the basis for the social sciences where its goal becomes the understanding of the total personality of man. It might be added that the Buddhist notion of existence is pervaded by emptiness and which understanding is made possible by the discovery of the concept of zero. Emptiness is the denial of any assertion relative to so-called metaphysical realities that may be imposed on man's nature, a denial which expresses a special feature of Buddhist thought. This feature cannot be absent in the study of man, as I have been reiterating with respect to the humanistic and social sciences.

Although Buddhism has the concept of emptiness, it is doubtful whether metaphysically oriented religions, such as Christianity, have discovered the concept of zero. It seems to me that in Christianity an absolute God occupies the place of emptiness. On this account, there is complete severance of ties between religion and philosophy. But since religion aims at the holistic consciousness of man, it cannot be classified as a true religion without this consciousness. This consciousness is akin to the love of God and refers, in the case of Buddhism, to the mutual ingression of the natures of wisdom (*prajñā*) and compassion (*karuṇā*).

It is extremely difficult, in terms of practicality, to judge whether it is good or bad for man and God to be in a state of complete severance. In a sense, it is within the province of religion to realize emptiness in order to aim at holistic consciousness. In the case of the philosophic study of man, however, it is mandatory that one becomes conscious of the unity of things in order to aim at holistic consciousness. Yet, if the two disciplines do not mutually ingress, it would not be possible to educe any real consciousness of the total nature of man founded on wisdom and compassion. On the other hand, from another aspect of things, in order to preserve the language in use, it may not be a bad idea to maintain the difference between the disciplines so that religion may preserve its purity. Although this seems to be admissible to some extent, since the one who expresses faith is still man, nevertheless, without proper understanding and philosophizing, strange phenomena may result, such as, a philosophy based on simply emulating certain personalities, or a sociology based on subjects cast as solitary personalities, severed from society itself. In either case, it is important that philosophy clearly distinguish between the realms of holistic consciousness (i.e., aspect of equality) and of discrimination (i.e., aspect of clarifying the boundaries of discourse).

It is said in Buddhism that one who teaches others with the presumption of *satori* (enlightenment) commits a most serious crime. One cannot be inconsistent with oneself, breaking away from holistic consciousness, but rather one must always acknowledge the boundaries of religion and philosophy. From the standpoint of total consciousness, religious consciousness should never be severed from everyday livelihood, a fact that only urges man to experientially embody this total consciousness.

Article 5

Emptiness and values in life are indeterminable matters but are so-called manifest secrets belonging to the realm of faith. Any analysis of them would invariably lead deeper and deeper into the agnostic realm, and yet, paradoxically, nothing would come to life without concretely embodying them. This is not to say that man could know everything by perceiving things scientifically, nor that he is in touch with the reality of life at all times, but to reveal the fact that everything is related to an aspect of infinity relative to time and space and that the whole of life cannot be neatly categorized in logical terms. In that situation, man constantly maintains an aspect of insecurity As problems arise, such as, on the infinity of life and values in conjunction with the concept of emptiness which can only be treated by way of understanding the realm of faith, it would be necessary to have a clear recognition of such a realm of existence.

Although in mathematics there are various theories on the concepts of zero and infinity, it would be nearly impossible today to philosophize them theoretically. Yet, we cannot merely abandon them as imponderables for the simple reason that experientially one knows that one lives in the present and that his life is enlivened by them.

The questions on the nature of life and death have been discussed variously in scientific circles and brought to bold relief by today's heart transplant operations. Theories aside, it behooves man to actualize his own temporal and spatial dimensions in essential ways. Though it is difficult for me to understand the full nature of life and death, nevertheless, they must become viable parts in one's life. Moreover, it is man's purpose in life to not only sustain himself but to carry and enliven everything else as he goes on living. Is this not the basis of the worth of an individual?

On the basis of such a purpose in life, a clear demarcation is allegedly made between religion and philosophy. But, by the same token, a kind of dialectical unity is established between the two. A word of caution is necessary here. In accepting things by virtue of the doctrine of nondiscriminative equality, one must guard against overreacting by treating religious doctrines in their nonrational forms directly to the actual social and scientific realms or by applying the evolutionary theory directly to the social evolutionary theory.

It is important then to clearly recognize the limits of discourse while maintaining at the same time a holistic consciousness. I do not sympathize with the view that science alone could solve everything, nor do I approve of the attitude that religion is extendable to any area including dabbling in such fields as economics and government.

It is man, not God, who experiences the world and who should be mindful of the limits of his own thinking process. It is frequently asserted that dialectic involves a transformation from quantity to quality or that all responsibility is left in the hands of God. But clearly that is not attributed to the basic principle of thinking by man.

Article 6

All concepts retain the dual standpoints of being and emptiness. In consequence, the truths on the conventional (*zokutai*; *saṃvṛti-sat*) and absolute (*shintai*; *paramārtha-sat*) levels mutually ingress, but, simultaneously, they are distinct. This condition is found only in Buddhist thought, a principle that is nowhere found in present Western thought. The principle, however, is easily accommodated in the natural sciences. But when it comes to the humanistic sciences, there will be great confusion if the conventional and absolute truths are not distinguished. Western philosophy today speaks with great concern on man's alienation, fragmentation, and deprivation of humanity, but the culprit, I believe, is in the inability to distinguish between the two truths. And the greatest confusion arises in the treatment and analysis of man, truth, and freedom. Philosophy, to be sure, treats such concepts, yet it fails to understand properly the difference between man and animal and the notion that the concept of man truly arises only through the educational process. Thus, it should be noted that, in order to prevent any confusion in the thinking process, the linguistic distinction between the two truths must be made clearly at the outset, i.e., between the concept of any man and the true nature of man. Nowadays, it is nearly impossible to have a clear answer to the question on the nature of man, truth, and freedom, a situation which seems to be the major cause of the confused state of affairs found in philosophy, as well as in social thought.

Lately, we hear the following asserted almost as a golden rule: "Heaven does not create anything beyond man," or the Cartesian "I think therefore I am." Now, if the terms in use are not clearly distinguished in regard to the nature of the two truths, they may undermine the very educational process. While imparting technical knowledge, the university is also a place where man is made, a place in constant search for the truth of existence. Unfortunately, it has been turned into a cruel place for examinations and has lost touch with the quest for the true nature of man. No wonder, then, that the very concept of a university is now called to question. We hear so often about the freedom of the university but then, what is meant by *freedom* of the university in the absence of the true nature of man?

The *Mahāparinirvāṇa Sūtra*, anticipating the confused state of affairs, expounds:[7]

> The ordinary sentient world is characterized by permanence, bliss, self and purity. The inordinate ('enlightenment') sentient world is also characterized by permanence, bliss, self and purity. The difference between the two is that although the ordinary world does not have truth but mere words, the inordinate world has both truth and words.

The passage clearly distinguishes between the conventional and absolute nature of truth, the latter of which incorporates the former.

In some circles today, man is hardly distinguished from animal; indeed, he is even substituted by the latter. This would be leaning toward the scientific analysis of everything, forgetting the distinction, and falling into the error of worshipping the sciences as the all powerful tool of investigation. But it is important to remind ourselves that philosophical investigation must begin with the distinction between the conventional and absolute nature of truth; indeed, the function of philosophy is the clarification of the two natures of truth.

The fundamental reason for the function of the dual truths lies in the fact that all concepts depend on the principle of dialectical

thinking whose two standpoints are being and emptiness. Expressed as a principle of equation, it is as follows:

$$a + b = c \qquad \text{(a, b, c represent beings or entities)}$$

$$(a + b) - c = 0$$

(all beings on the left equal to the total
empty state which, paradoxically, depicts
the full accommodaton of all beings)

Now, how is man able to take on the two standpoints? The
reason is simple. It lies in the fact that the self is able to see itself
from the standpoint of 'nonstandpoint', i.e., from the absolute
standpoint, where there is total or holistic consciousness — the
standpoint of absolute nature of man. As an extension, we might
add that to learn the essence of emptiness from the sciences is the
function of true scientific philosophy.

Article 7

The following assertions can be made. For a single vision or eye-
consciousness, there will always be a limitation. Therefore, it
would prevent the rise of any superstructural ('transcendental')
nature of things. Moreover, the leap ('transformation') from quantity to quality is in the nature of a logical leap and not a physical or
material one.

In the *Heart Sūtra*, the explanation of the various sense faculties
(eye, ear, nose, tongue, body, and mind) with respect to their corresponding sense objects (eye-object, ear-object, etc.) is represented by the single example of eye-consciousness to indicate the
consummation of sense experience. Consequently, the so-called six
internal sense organs, six external objects relative to the sense
organs, and six consciousnesses which consummate the six organs
and their objects always stand in the relationship of contradictory
self-unity (or antinomical self-identity). The fundamental principle
of epistemology expressed here means that no correct perception
(or cognition) is possible by focussing on only one aspect or phase
of the sense experience. This principle, extended in detail to other
areas, would mean that if, for instance, the world is seen under
economic eyes, then everything will appear in the realm of
economics; if seen under political eyes, everything will appear in
the realm of politics; and, if seen under scientific eyes, everything

will appear in the realm of matter, but all are narrow limited views. Furthermore, under this principle, what is known as materialism will be just another form of conceptualism. It would certainly be arbitrary to take economics as the basis for the construction of higher strata of society, such as, in terms of government, laws, and culture, for it would be a mere arbitrary judgment that cannot be used to establish the foundations of the educational process.

We must be extremely cautious in dealing with the learning process by not going astray. As the educational realm is illimitable, should there be a slight deviation, it would be like entering a thousand miles of thicket. In such a situation, what is needed is to develop the total (holistic) consciousness of being. It calls for a dialectical consciousness, since all learning is within man's enterprise and any phase of it is part and parcel of the total consciousness. Without this consciousness, delusions of all kinds will begin to appear, such as, reducing everything to materialism or treating man in terms of science. And such delusions will not only be limited to individuals but will involve everyone in the world.

It would be quite easy to extend the nature of the individual self, as it is, to be man's consciousness or to think that one's own asserted principle is the best and thereby incorporate and subsume everything else. But this is a most dangerous trap to fall into, and in order to avoid it one must always take on the perspective of the Buddhist nature of non-self (*muga; anātman*) to reflect upon things. One must also keep in mind that the non-self perspective is actually a special privilege open to man which shows the way to the realization of total consciousness.

Incidentally, we find similar instances of man's weakness in the various peace proposals. That is to say, a would-be peaceful world has no chance of actualizing itself simply because there is no self-realization of the trap one has fallen into, which not only impedes the peace process but creates further confusion. It seems to me that such a reflection is best exemplified in the *Seventeen-Article Constitution* by Prince Shōtoku (573–621 A.D.). The famous Tenth Article states:[8]

> Let us cease from wrath, and refrain from angry looks. Nor let us be resentful when others differ from us. For all men have hearts, and each heart has its own leanings. Their right is our wrong, and our right is their wrong. We are not unquestionably sages, nor are

they unquestionably fools. Both of us are simply ordinary men. How can any one lay down a rule by which to distinguish right from wrong? For we are all, one with another, wise and foolish, like a ring which has no end. Therefore, although others give way to anger, let us on the contrary dread our own faults, and though we alone may be in the right, let us follow the multitude and act like them.

This is a profound teaching based on the realization of the total consciousness of man and guided by the Buddhist Three Treasures, i.e., the Buddha (enlightened state of existence), the Dharma (truth of existence), and the Sangha (assemblage of aspirants of truth). To those who are unable to realize the total consciousness, the Article will be read as just another vague statement on human relationship.

It would seem clear, regardless of the issues, which side is the real democratic way of life that respects other individuals: those who demand self-criticism on the part of professors and presidents, or those who self-reflect as a result of listening to the views of opponents. On the other hand, there are those who fall into the democratic trap, arbitrarily judging democracy to be the best form of government, the alpha and omega of life and who are unable thereby to perceive things clearly concerning the nature of plain truth. This is a grave pitfall of the educational process, a delusory way of education which even escapes common sense. Although there is an initial distinction made between common sense and education, it should be kept in mind that both are not separated completely and are constantly in a dialectical relationship.

Article 8

Body, speech, and will are essentially a single act (gō; *karma*) in which they mutually interpenetrate. In consequence, any work or activity is not simply a matter of time.

It can be said that Western thought is fundamentally based on the contrasting nature between concepts and things. In Buddhism, however, everything is distinguished into the three aspects of body, speech, and will in which man is considered to be the 'subject' arising from his own acts. In this way, man's subjectivity and responsibility are clearly defined. The sense of responsibility does not arise so long as one is caught up in a surrounding described by conceptions, matter, God, and nature which have no relationship to his deeds. Should one fall into such an existence, willy nilly obeying the laws of nature or the commands of God, then one would be actually unrelated to God, as well as society at large. One's sense of responsibility would be sacrificed on that account. In this way, a completely different way of thinking exists in the West which is oriented toward individual deeds within a surrounding.

In Eastern (Buddhist) thought, the acts or deeds of the body, speech, and will are all combined, i.e., 'three therefore one', or 'one therefore three,' an instance of dialectical integration, namely the *logic of unity*. Bodily act is always accompanied (potentially) by the acts of speech and will; speech act, in turn, is accompanied (potentially) by the acts of body and will; and finally, the will is accompanied (potentially) by the acts of the body and speech. In this way, the three separate acts can be thought of as basically a single act. In Buddhism, the three acts are condensed to the five sense faculties and the mind, all of which express *in toto* the nature of existence or sense experience.

In Western thought, by contrast, all of existence is framed within the context of concepts and things and a clear demarcation made between the two, i.e., no things in concepts, and, vice versa, no concepts in things. This situation ignores the fact that man is a dialectical unity and promotes instead a way of thinking that is antilearning. That is, it would reduce everything to a simple realism in which mere existence is admitted but the possibility of establishing a cognitive process based on treating realities without any rules of inference is denied.

Take the further example of what is a speech act — is it mere language, words, or symbols? Is a language a 'thing'? Or, is it in the nature of the mind? Without defining the nature of the speech act, steadfastly maintaining a cut and dried separation between concepts and things, would invariably result in a situation considered to be noneducational and nonscientific. Since such an unscientific epistemology would not foster real philosophizing, Buddhism, for that reason, will not arbitrarily distinguish between mind and matter. If one were to conclude too hastily that there are only concepts and things, then one would be caught in a dilemma: either derive any meaning from symbols or attribute any meaning to symbols. In short, the initial dichotomy forecloses any later attempts at seeking the unity of experience.

Take the following statement: "The emperor is the symbol of national unity." It would be extremely difficult to explain it to people who fail to understand it as an expression based on the logic of unity. To those who have total holistic consciousness, on the other hand, it would readily be understood in the sense that the nation is one's own country or the house is one's own home.

It is necessary that all living persons have a face. Can someone, for example, who aims at fostering practical matters, assert that man only requires the head and limbs but no features and forms? A face, after all, is not something that merely fills a space but is an undeniable vital symbolic expression of integration, i.e., an integrated experience. The face does not perform a function, to be sure, in the sense of the head. Nor does it do the work of the limbs. It seems to be a most useless and boring part of the whole body, taken organically. It may well be that the mouth or nose could have been attached to some other parts of the body without destroying their function. Even man-made food tubes or respiratory pipes very well could be installed. Ironically, though, we attach the greatest value to this seemingly useless face. But it is only human, as we are accustomed to say, to protect the face as much as possible from injury while other parts of the body may sustain injuries. Why is this so? There seems to be something selfish and delimiting in our attitudes and actions.

Be that as it may, is it not the case that the concept of responsibility refers to the total integrated act that involves the body, speech and will? Man's act, therefore, cannot be treated merely on surface, like facial expressions, for the nature of freedom and responsibility are deeply rooted in his being.

Article 9

The open mind allows complete interpenetration of elements to mold a free personality. When the mind is closed, there arises the realm of ignorance and delusion which becomes the basis for universal suffering.

The above statement is the historical view of freedom in Buddhism, the expression or interruption of the doctrine of twelvefold

interrelational origination. It is indeed rare to find another doctrine like it which has been so thoroughly interpreted over the ages
by different schools and sects. It expounds in essence the principle
of self-act self-realization, that the history (life) of man is a series
of determinations based on free acts. It is, in short, an explanation
of the development of man's unique individuality.

In the nature of development, it is recognized that there is a difference in explanation between psychological ontogeny and embryological ontogeny. In the case of the individual's deterministic
and developmental natures, however, the doctrine of interrelational origination explains the growth in terms of the individual's
imprisonment to the concept of self relative to the unconscious attachment to its passions. It also depicts the path trodden by ordinary person's hell-like existence and, at the same time, expounds
on the reverse enlightened view (*paṭiloma*) of the doctrine of interrelational origination which amounts to the famous Fourfold Noble
Truth. The doctrine essentially has those two facets. In sum, then,
man has the tendency to fall into the path of depravity if he does not
properly educate himself. Conversely, should he properly educate
himself, he would enter the holistic realm of *satori*, thus confirming
the historical nature of freedom and realizing Buddha-nature while
still existing within the matrix of the will bound in ignorance or
delusion. This view is directly opposed to historical determinism
based on Marxian historical materialism. Needless to say, all of
this becomes patently clear in light of reason and does not really
require further explanation.

Accordingly, compared with Marxian determinism, the Buddhist historical view of man is a treatise on freedom. The only pro-
vision is that in Buddhism there would be an inevitable fall into
depravity should man fail to understand the fundamental principle
involved in the doctrine of interrelational origination. Thus, if
there is an imposition of metaphysical beliefs on the social sciences
and no recognition of their limitations, it would be analogous to
treading the same steps as one who unwillingly follows the dictates
of God's prophecy.

Article 10

Man (his character), truth, and freedom, from the standpoint
of absolute truth, constitute a conception which manifests the dia-

lectically interpenetrated nature of things and form the basis of a proper view of man and society.

As a proper logic is necessary to delve into the nature of man and for the understanding of nature as such, the model of such a logic is found in natural mathematics. Therein, in turn, is discovered the principles of correct thinking, the dialectic. Moreover, by extending the function of dialectic to general concepts, it is possible to determine a proper epistemology. In so doing, finally, we were able to obtain the valuable key in pursuit of the fundamental question, "What is man?"

In dialectic, i.e., in the forms of $a + b = c$ and $(a + b) - c = 0$, we were able to discern the patterns involved for what we refer to as truth, freedom, and total holistic consciousness. Furthermore, we are able to discern a correct view of society by applying dialectic to its various groups.

By establishing the basis of human reason, it is possible to demonstrate the continuity in the truths expressed in the natural sciences and philosophy, including the social sciences; moreover, although the truths in religion and philosophy seem to form a continuity, there are also discontinuous elements which then express certain limitations between the two disciplines.

The confusion in philosophy today can be attributed to the fact that a premature type of logic has been extended to the most basic concepts of freedom, truth, and man.

On the basis of the above assertions, we are able to affirm the belief and general consensus of a rational basis underlying the natural sciences and the essential nature of man. And by means of the dialectic, we are able to know that the conclusions found in the *Mahāparinirvāṇa Sūtra* are in general agreement with the four pillars of the *Japanese Constitution*, including the educational goals expressed in the Japanese Basic Law of Education.

In this way, then, the most difficult Buddhist principles were explained by means of the principles derived in the natural mathematics. We were able to realize, at the same time, the fact that Buddhist thought manifests the highest form of man's reason and expresses what we today refer to as the science of man. It should be noted that the social sciences in the future cannot ignore this science of man. Moreover, there is a firm conviction that Buddhist thought, serving as a basis for the social sciences, is a most unique doctrine.

Conclusions

The problem which is causing the greatest confusion on the foundation of social education is what may be referred to as 'contemporary consciousness'. This consciousness is allegedly another way of expressing 'man's limited consciousness'. Although it is given significant focus in the contemporary scene, paradoxically, it expresses the present confused state of affairs.

I am not at all attempting to construct a new philosophy. Nor am I combatting capitalism or socialism, nor seeking to prove the supremacy of Buddhism or Christianity or Judaism. Rather, I only wish to assert that, in this new era, one must affirm the distinctive subjective nature of man by transcending the views on him attributed to the religious traditions and must start anew in this democratic age with à firm basis in social education. I also believe that, although we pay due respect to the three great religions of Buddhism, Christianity, and Judaism, at the same time, we must aspire for a basis of thought that transcends all of them.

We can meet the challenge by reversing the general methodology used in past social sciences research. It is here that the simple rudiments of mathematics were introduced to expedite an understanding of the methodology. In the past, however, this type of demonstrative truth form was probably not employed in philosophy proper.

It is important for us to judge what is proper as proper and what is improper as improper. Although information accumulates by leaps and bounds on a daily basis, the power of judgment must be present as the fundamental basis of social education. In this world, there are those who spend a lifetime collecting data for judgment, but being mere intellectual worms, they are unable to achieve an enlightened state of existence. There are those, on the other hand, who may be dim on general knowledge but who possess the important power of judgment to sift the proper from the improper nature of things.

Proper judgments do not arise out of a vacuum, for they require the maintenance of a firm standard. This standard is actually in the nature of truth. There are many factors involved in instituting the standard. For example, God may be the standard or even nature. In recent years, however, science itself has become a standard for all judgments, delineating a clear case of the takeover by scientism.

Although philosophy treats the most crucial questions in man, things that are most intimate to the masses, paradoxically, philosophers are noted for engaging in abstruse expositions on matters that are considered most simple. On the other hand, religion attempts to explain matters in simple terms, vulgarizing matters in the process to such an extent that it invites superstitious elements to enter.

Thus, what is close to all and what is discernible as the truth must be prevalent not merely as a question in philosophy but as a vital foundation of social education. That was the inception of the method adopted, i.e., the one that used simple arithmetic, as it is, as the standard of judgment. Man is endowed a priori with the power of judging good from evil and right from wrong, but that is so because it is only necessary to have knowledge of simple arithmetic functions to determine the basis of judgment. Difficult matters may be entrusted to experts, but simple matters ought not to be tangled in abstruse language. It is only necessary to have the wisdom to distinguish between what should be left to the experts and what to the judgment of ordinary people.

What is necessary in man's discernment is always to look for the mountain, as it were. In this vein, a saying goes as follows: "the hunter preys on the deer but does not look at the mountain," a saying that depicts a myopic vision, a situation not uncommon in educational circles.

Notwithstanding the use of arithmetic function in Buddhism, its use in explaining dialectical movement probably never had been done before. As arithmetic itself is a kind of symbolic logic, its function is already inherent to the nature of formal logic, as well as to dialectical logic. It is therefore quite odd that, up to the present, arithmetic had not been related to problems in philosophy and logic. Arithmetic was not invented by anyone. It is actually the product of a very long history, as old as the history of language in human terms with a symbolic nature attested to by countless numbers of people.

Truth itself is also not something created by someone and forced upon others in authoritarian ways, but it is ideally found, causing the least amount of doubt, from within the long historical experience of man. On this point, it can be said that mathematical dialectic is richest among dialectics in the nature of experiential evidences. As the basis of general social education, it is undoubtedly the most attractive dialectic favored by all. Its closeness to Hegelian dialectic or Marxian dialectic or even Buddhist dialectic aside, it can be thought of as the most propitious basis for a dialogue between Eastern and Western mind.

Further Analysis of the Ten Articles

(As an afterthought to the analysis of the above ten articles, the author has appended a further analysis on them. Although it contains new ideas and new slants in amplification of the articles, it also covers old grounds. But, rather than editing them, I have left them as they are to retain the author's original intent and spirit. In any event, they are valuable and significant additions to the understanding of key concepts. — Trans.)

Holistic consciousness

On the basis of instituting the nature of philosophy governed by various principles, the answer to the question "What is man?" has turned out to be extremely diverse, conflicting, and indeed confusing. The situation has become worse in the contemporary period. While it is difficult to demarcate between modern and contemporary thought, my feelings are that contemporary thought has the special characteristic of the absence of the concept of man'.

Friedrich Nietzsche made the famous pronouncement, "God is dead." But I will go further to assert simultaneously that "man too is dead." The loss of God in Western thought concurrently signifies the loss of man.

Since man becomes man through education, the question "What is man?" is naturally vastly different from other similarly posed questions, such as, "What is a cat?" or "What is a tiger?" But, in the exploration into linguistic analysis in contemporary philosophy, what philosophic contents there are initially would inevitably evaporate into sheer nothingness. As we are not merely in the business of doing research in zoology or in technology for that matter, we should never forget the fact that man is an educable quantity. This is not to focus on the biological nature of man but on "What is the nature of an educated man?"

All this brings the discussion to what I meant by the phrase 'holistic consciousness'. The total nature of the sciences refers to every aspect that runs to the illimitable far corners of the world. There is not a single science in the world which is unrelated to the nature of man. Holistic consciousness, therefore, is that consciousness which is at one with the total (nature of) world, the only true consciousness in man.

Dialectic is found where man and the world have become one, where one's self has returned to the unity of things, i.e., united with respect to the conception of one's country, one's home, and one's neighbor. This dialectic, when analyzed, refers to the total widsom (*prajñā*) in man, but, when the phenomenon is considered in the total unified sense, it refers to the deepest love or compassion (*karuṇā*).

In Article 1, the dialectic was presented in the form of the mathematical principle that infinite numbers do not lose their individualities and that the consciousness in accord with the principle issuing forth 'totality as unity' is identical to man's true consciousness. This does not deviate at all from the Buddhist doctrine of interrelational origination which is the basis of total nature of wisdom (*issaichi*; *sarvajñata*), as well as total nature of love (*issaiai* or *jihi*; *karuṇā*).

This total wisdom corrects the waywardness of our fancies and dreams. Man's conduct, naturally, cannot be related to the total nature of things at all times; yet, however small the segment of the experiential whole one is engaged in one should not lose touch with the fact that the segment is clearly part and parcel of the totality. This is the way to prevent one from falling into fancies or dreamy states of existence.

When ordinary man loses the power of self-restraint, he easily deludes himself into thinking that he, alone, is the whole of being and that such delusory examples have continued from a distant past. Such rampant and slanted views as "the chosen people," "the divine wind," "man is not a man unless he is from the Taira clan," or the prewar military syndicalism, postwar university syndicalism and other group syndicalism, are all based on the failure to comprehend the true nature of total human consciousness and of democratic principles.

Dialectic

The second article had discussed the fundamental form of the dialectic based on holistic consciousness of principles and laws applicable to units and things. To the question, "Why is dialectic the truth of the nature of things?" the following can be asserted: the truth of the nature of things takes the form of an equation in mathematical logic that reveals itself in ordinary logic as a dialectic or, as mentioned earlier, as the function of the Buddhist doctrine of interrelational origination. At the same time, we must dispense with past metaphysical thinking that merely accepts truth as something based on dialectic and return to a more fundamental standpoint by raising such questions as, "What is dialectic?" "What is the function of dialectic?" and "In what manner should dialectical materialism or dialectical idealism manifest?" By the introduction of this form of mathematical dialectic, it is hoped that any separate treatment of natural truths and philosophical truths would be avoided and that their similarities, as well as differences, would be rendered clear.

Prior to Hegel in Western thought, the basic category of truth was not called to question. Even today, unfortunately, God and truth are still thought in some quarters to be in the same category, and it is thought that philosophy's aim and purpose are not in quest of the earthly human-oriented truth but an indirect reference to the reality of truth based on the demonstration of God's existence. This trend in the contemporary world still rings loud with metaphysical overtones. Even after Hegel, when the category of truth had shifted somewhat, the idea that truth must be tied in with the concept of God or Nature lingered, and Western thought could not completely shake itself from the notion of God and truth as forms of being. It could not start *de novo*, as in Eastern thought, from the standpoint of man's nature of reason per se to perceive the nature of things.

Since Christianity, fortunately, developed as a world religion in which the nature of its God started with the Jewish God of wrath and ended with the God of love, it has an excellent overall management of human affairs; yet, precisely on this account, it could not satisfy human reason and thus brought about the present

dichotomy between religion and philosophy. With the maintenance of the fundamental separation between God and man
and the insistence on the concept of God as a being, there is hardly
any chance that fate would overturn everything and cause the so-
called discovery of the zero. In consequence, even in Western
philosophy, the discovery of the zero did not occur but, seriously,
can we permit the distorted truth to linger forever under the sway
of God's dispensation?

Dialectical epistemology

The third article offered a solution to the problem of applying dialectic to the realm of general conceptions. That is to say, as there are
unknown quantities everywhere in the equations with respect to
the four basic operations $(+, -, \times, \div)$ of natural numbers, just so
there are untold numbers of questions relative to human existence.
Correspondingly, the four basic operations may be expanded to
the algebraic realm whose unknown quantities may, in turn, be expanded to the realm of general conceptions. The expansion ex-
poses the original form inherent in the dialectic which was then
disclosed in terms of principles. As evidence of the foregoing, one
may point to any language which inevitably has the subject-verb
construct, i.e., in the nature of 'it is . . . ', which demonstrates the
fact that man's thinking process does not differ in form to the
nature of mathematical logic or ordinary logic.

In Western philosophy from the past, there has been an opposition between dialectical materialism and dialectical idealism or
conceptualism. But as dialectic must be the principle that underlies
all thought process, as well as existence, both principle and object
must mutually ingress to form a proper cognition. Thus, to argue
whether the mathematical form is matter or spirit would even
arouse the curiosity of a grade school child. The determination of
the problem lies in the treatment of subjective consciousness, i.e.,
whether it is taken as a mere conceptual problem or a more inclusive and holistic existential problem.

Discovery of philosophical zero

In pursuing the question further, it is only natural that we con-
front such problems as the concepts of 'zero' and 'infinity' which

do not surface openly in Western dialectic. These problems were exhaustively treated in the Buddhist context. That is, in Buddhism, the 'zero' and 'infinity' were treated as 'emptiness' (*kū, śūnyatā*) in order to transcend the category of 'being' or of all so-called realities. It also proves, I believe, that there is no solution forthcoming from a philosophy based on the concept of 'being' or 'substance' and that such present day systems as materialism or positivism exhibit the inadequacy of understanding the principle of man's thinking.

Dialectic of religion and philosophy

The fifth article pursued the extremely difficult question of values and the concept of emptiness in Western thought. It went further to state that, since man is to be considered neither as an animal nor a machine, there is no philosophy apart from religion and, vice versa, no religion apart from philosophy. Yet, it was made abundantly clear that the relationship between the two disciplines is strictly dialectical such that neither the realm of faith nor the question of faith itself should be affected indiscriminately as a theoretical or logical problem.

Principle of dual truths

As stated earlier, the basic principle of dialectic is inherent to the mathematical equations: $a + b = c$ and $(a + b) - c = 0$. The first equation is a dialectic based on the concept of being and the second on emptiness, i.e., a reflective form of dialectic. Together they inform that all conceptions are formed dialectically and each conception takes on a dual nature of being and emptiness. This is quite necessary for the listener to bear in mind in communication. Buddhism from the outset had clearly distinguished between the nature of conventional (provisional) and absolute truths, a distinction not clearly understood in Western thought.

Accordingly, it is important to be very strict on the definition and use of words. But, aside from genuine philosophic discourse which must maintain the strictness, ordinary conversation as a rule breaks down, unable to keep up with the strict use of terms, the consequence of which is conventional use and relevance to conventional truth only. Even in contemporary thought, the most difficult definitions, such as those on man, truth, freedom, character, and consciousness—all of which belong to the realm of social sciences—have been reduced to conventional truth. In consequence, it should be noted that these definitions, in their strictness and directness to truth, are important and necessary in discussing the nature of Eastern wisdom.

That a conception is able to take on two standpoints means that man himself can take on the dual positions of being and emptiness and that he has the power to separate (transcend) from his own being in order to see himself fully. This standpoint is none other than the unique perspective delineated in the doctrine of non-self which is conspicuously absent in Western thought. In consequence, in the West there is very little emphasis on the self-reflective nature of things. The principle of self-reflection, however, is quite significant and fundamental to mathematical dialectic. It may be said to be a basic principle in hermeneutic or interpretive sciences, and, incidentally, there are occasions in which the conceptions of the humanistic sciences are able to convey intentions without giving way to materialistic connotations. Because of this, when viewing things from the standpoint of emptiness, the self has transcended itself and viewing in this fashion becomes an inalienable principle that retains proper subjective judgment.

Unitary dialectic and integrative dialectic

The seventh and eighth articles have shown the use of dialectic in the case of a single conception and in the case of its carry over to man's practical affairs in concrete integrative ways. From the standpoint of Buddhist thought, it means that mind and matter—concepts and things—are not easily or clearly distinguishable.

Both materialistic and conceptualistic dialectic, without a well-defined terminology, are concepts readily used in extremely conventional (common sense) ways. When they are brought before the real nature of a dialectic, however, it is shown that they constitute a unitary dialectic, as well as an integrative dialectic; moreover, in the realm of the practical, logical, and conscious, a dialectic is well-established. And it is clear that one cannot speak about man's total activity in mere physical terms without involving his speech and consciousness to round out his total realm of existence.

These two articles have then attempted to narrow down the meaning and definition of both materialistic and conceptualistic dialectic through the function of mathematical logic.

Dialectical historicism

The question whether history is guided by freedom or necessity is a huge problem in present Western thought. The dialectical historicism expounded here is exactly identical to the consequences yielded in the Buddhist doctrine of twelvefold interrelational origination. This doctrine spells out that, when man's total holistic consciousnes is present, the historical process would be free, but, when it is absent, man would fall into the realm of ignorance and invariably revert to necessity. As Buddhist teaching says, "What one reaps accords with what one sows,"[9] similarly, historical process is in the nature of one's own responsibility. All this is vastly different from the Marxian metaphysical determinism, i.e., historical materialism based on economics.

Conception of life and world view

Since dialectic is a basic principle applicable to both individual and group, being man's basic way of thinking, it is only natural that man's conception of life be regulated by his proper attitudes. In other words, by placing the whole ten articles together, it would be possible to answer such basic questions as "What is man?" or "What is man's consciousness?," the result being the proper consciousness of man's conception of life and his world.

The ten articles, in general conceptual terms, may then be subtitled man's conception of life and the world. They are not merely limited to religious and logical questions but extend to the principles of social sciences, such as, political science, economics, law, and so on—all of which focus on the science of man. This means that in essence the science of man is the sine qua non in social education, and thus there is no necessity of philosophizing in any specialized way. Since data have been accumulating from past experiences, it only requires a standard of judgment to make proper selections, a standard on the application of certain datum for a certain situation and on the proper perception and thinking of things. This standard is sorely lacking in present day social education.

The standard in social education must be based on a principle clearly evident to everyone. It must be a type of an open philosophy, one that has the character of a philosophy of philosophy, clearly seen and grasped by all. It should not be one that is selected from among existing philosophies but one that stands aloof from all systems and is based on its own merits or principles. For this reason, we made the standard of thinking to be the rudimentary mathematical function established over a long history of man.

We believe we have advanced the exposition closer to our projected goals. As evidence, we may take up the discussion of the *Daimuryōjukyō (Mahāsukhāvatī vyuha-sūtra; The Land of Bliss)*.[10] In it there is a discussion of the six so-called divine powers (*saḍ-abhijñāḥ*). These powers were realized by the Buddha when he was enlightened or gained total holistic consciousness. They are the powers to transcend ordinary man's perception, such as, the power to recall the status of former existence, to perceive the future status of existence, to hear more than the ordinary sounds, to understand other person's thought, to tread wherever one wishes, and to rid oneself of all defilements or obstacles of existence.

In more specific terms, the first divine power refers to the ability to understand the reason for one's existence as a human being, in short, to know one's nature of being. In present language, it addresses the problem of man's conception of life. The second divine power refers to the ability to perceive other enlightened realms (i.e., the Buddha lands). In present language, it refers I believe to the attainment of proper social and world views. The third, in present language, refers to the ability to hear a teaching without the reliance on vocal sounds, i.e., to hear the Buddha's teachings by 'deciphering' the message in the already existing total phenomena of society. The fourth refers to the ability to know the mind of another person or, in modern terms, to know the exact nature and position of an idea or thought within the context of the various ways of thinking in the world. This is only natural by virtue of the fact that one has grasped the true total holistic consciousness and thereby the content of what is man. The previously stated adage, "The hunter preys on the deer but does not look at the mountain," is commonly acknowledged. But, in actuality, we ought to know exactly where the hunter is stalking the deer relative to the humanly constructed mountain. The fifth refers to the ability to traverse the land of many Buddhas in a single thought moment. In modern terms, it means that, although there are many ways to express the goal of life, it should be possible to distinguish any and all of the ways freely in that single thought moment. The sixth, finally, refers to the fact that, to people of the Buddha land which involves all of us, true consciousness will not be realized in the presence of defilements, but there should be, at the same time, infinite faith and resolve that those defilement-ridden persons will be released in the end.

In such a way the *Daimuryōjukyō* expounds on the nature of total holistic consciousness and its underlying dialectic. It should be added that these six divine powers have been discussed throughout the whole of Buddhism, starting with the *Four Nikāyas*[11] in early Bubbhism and continuing on into the Mahāyāna tradition where the quest for the true nature of man has expanded in a truly practical, all-encompassing, and reflexive way.

Chapter III

The Truth in the *Heart Sūtra*

On the methodology of comparative philosophy, I have presented the conceptions of 'realization of the mind-base' and its contrary 'intuitive unconsciousness'—tension between consciousness and ignorance (*avidyā*)—by relying on geometric schemes and natural mathematical equations. This was expressed on the basis of dimensional forms (constructs) by comparing Eastern analysis of psychological structures (five *skandhas* are all empty) with the Western psychological analytic scheme (senses, intellect, and reason). Now I would like to pursue further and focus on the methodology of comparative philosophy by reference to a most elementary but basic text of the East, *Prajñāpāramitāhrdaya Sūtra* (*Heart Sūtra*), and to demonstrate, therefrom, the fact that philosophy and the natural sciences or philosophy and theology are all based on the concept of Dharma (truth of existence) and invariably return to the doctrine of One Mind.

Although the *Heart Sūtra* is composed of a mere 260 words (Chinese characters), it is actually based on the bulky *Mahāprajñāpāramitā Sūtra* in 600 fascicles[1] but the 260 words represent the essence (hence, heart) of the above work. While each word is weighty, involving volumes in comments, the *Sūtra* itself is trusted and revered, since it records the truthful transmission of the Dharma down through the ages in traditions both internal and external.

103

'Through the ages' refers to the period from early Buddhism to present day Mahāyāna Buddhism, and 'internal and external' depict Japan and foreign countries, as well as Far Eastern and Western thought. In asserting the above, we are compelled to add that the *Heart Sūtra* did not find its way to the West until modern times and that, aside from the Bible, there is not a single work which represents Western thought in terms of a singular thought pattern. The Bible, however, is a work of faith and should not be confused with a philosophy or an idea. On the other hand, by expounding the truth of existence transmitted in the *Heart Sūtra*, it should become clear that many ideas of the West will have an affinity to it and, at the same time, hopefully, prompt some serious self-reflection on the part of Western thought. This is what was meant by the statement in reference to the truthful transmission of the truth of existence both internally and externally. Accordingly, I will not analyze Western philosophical truth in order to compare it with the truth found in the *Heart Sūtra*. Instead, I would like to bring everything together and comparatively examine the basic opposing views of Eastern and Western philosophy.

The *Heart Sūtra* is an extremely important but common text which is even recited by many people. According to the *Kaigenroku*,[2] an old historical work, the famous Hsüan-tsang, on May 24th of the year 649 A.D., translated this sutra at the detached palace in the Chung-nan-shan (mountain), and it was subsequently handed down by his disciples. I will use this simple version.

It should be noted at the outset that I am not attempting to expound the sutra for literary concern or religious intentions but only because, from the standpoint of comparative philosophy, it is essential in ideological analysis to pursue accurately what is the nature of truth. In taking such an approach, however, there is always the danger of being considered outside the mainstream of academic circles for indulging in things that are deemed nonacademic and nonphilosophical. But it would seem to me that today's philosophy and certain ideological systems have the knack of pursuing any text or literature in a highly specialized sense, researching into the minutest matter, but seem lacking in taking on the higher and broader view of things. On this point, I might add, the intuitive and nonanalytic nature of Zen is much closer to philosophy itself and readily shows the fruitful path to the truth of things.

Once a monk in China inquired of his master, "What was the situation before the arrival of Bodhidharma from the West?" To which the master replied, "99, 81." The monk persevered further, "What was the situation after the arrival of Bodhidharma from the West?" To which the master replied, "66, 36." It is obvious that both replies are illogical and absurd. The point is that, regardless of whether Bodhidharma came or did not come from India, the status of the unchanging truth of things remains; in the same vein, whether the Buddha apeared or did not appear in this world is absolutely irrelevant to the truth of things which has existed so solemnly from time immemorial, but, of course, the Buddha did realize it (Dharma). Buddhism is actually the capture of this consciousness of the truth (Dharma) whose sustaining spirit has not changed in the development of the various schools from early (primitive) Buddhism to the Mahāyāna.

The late Christmas Humphreys of the London Buddhist Society has a book entitled *Buddhism*. In it the following dialogue is recorded.[3]

Question: "What is Buddhism?"
Answer: "Buddhism is the name given by the Westerner to the doctrine expounded by Śākyamuni. The East, from olden times, have referred to it as the Buddhist Dharma."

Indeed the *Heart Sūtra* captures the essence of the Buddhist Dharma in extremely clear and concise manner.

We may in a sense say that all learning today is entirely the search of the truth of existence. Yet, how many are able to answer in less than 260 words such questions as, "What is the truth?" "What is philosophy?" "What is Man?" "What is God?" and "What is the Buddha?" The *Heart Sūtra* naturally expounds on these questions in its own way.

Come to think of it, there are many throughout the world who are seekers of the truth, but, admittedly, there are but a few who realize it. Man must, of course, be pious and relentless in the search, for only those who are dedicated and serious enough can hope to succeed. Judging philosophy and ideology today, it would seem that they are permeated and influenced greatly by value judgments, such as, pointing at the old and the new. This is not only limited to the common sense realm but pervades the whole realm of learning. What is more, it has been taken to be the natural thing to do. But truth itself has no newness or oldness; it is eternal and unchanging in any situation even as it marches off outside of a particular tradition. The *Heart Sūtra,* needless to say, accommodates such a situation.

The *Heart Sūtra* (*Prajñāpāramitāhṛdaya-sūtra*)

Let us begin with the sutra's name. The sutra is commonly prefixed with the term *Mahā* or *Buddhavacana* (Buddha's teachings). *Mahā* means great, which was later attached to the sutra to give it the sense of solemnity or majesty. The Indian Sanskrit original has it as *Prajñāpāramitāhṛdaya Sūtra* which in Japanese is phonetically rendered as *Hannyaharamita-shingyō*. *Prajñā* refers to the three forms of knowledge by means of listening, reasoning, and practicing, all of which collectively consummates in wisdom which is different and deeper than ordinary intelligence. *Pāramitā* refers to the crossing over to the other shore, from ignorance to enlightenment or from the mundane existence to the Buddhist realm of *satori*. Thus the sutra, in entirety, may be interpreted as focussing on the enlightened mind.

The word sutra was added later, creating some confusion as to whether it depicts the essence of Buddhism as such or of the whole 600 fascicles *Mahāprajñāpāramitā Sūtra*. In reality, it should be considered to depict the identity of the consciousness of truth and the term *prajñāpāramitāhṛdaya*, the essence of the enlightened truth. The consciousness of truth is, at once, the consciousness of the Dharma, for in Buddhism the Dharma is identical to the consciousness of the truth. All of this points to the essence of the teachings found in the *Mahāprajñāpāramitā Sūtra*, and it would not be remiss to consider it as the pivotal text in Mahāyāna Buddhism.

In Buddhism, the so-called wisdom of *prajñā* or *prajñā*-wisdom is explained from both the aspect of reality as such and the aspect of clear perception of reality. More specifically, reality is the principle of *prajñā* and clear perception, the wisdom of *prajñā*. In Western philosophy, they correspond roughly to the realms of ontology and epistemology, but the reality expressed in the *Heart Sūtra* refers to the reality of the mind in the context of *prajñā*. This reality resides with man and, on this point, diverges greatly and importantly from the Western ontological view which generally posits reality external to man.

If the wisdom and rational basis of *prajñā* are expressed in or by words, it would constitute mere 'literary *prajñā*'. Even Kitarō Nishida in his *Zen-no-kenkyū* (A Study of Good), Part II, Chapter 2, states that "conscious phenomena constitute unique reality."[4] The question of whether reality resides in or out of man thus marks the fundamental split between Eastern (Buddhist) philosophy and Western philosophy. The key to comparative philosophy from the Eastern standpoint could be seen in the simple assertion, "The five aggregates of being are all empty," which clearly expresses the nature of the reality of the total mind.

In my methodology, the reality achieved in *prajñā* has been schematized as the 'realization of the mind-base'. The fact that 'all is empty' cannot be consciously known, due to its nature of deep psychological stratum, has been labelled 'intuitive unconscious'. In the realization of the mind-base, however, there is both intuitive function and an unconscious nature of 'empty characteristics.' But the dual nature has generated the difference between the enlightened (Buddha) and the unenlightened (ordinary sentient being), issuing forth further the difference between right and wrong, between truth and falsity.

In what follows, according to the order of treatment in the *Heart Sūtra*, I would like to raise such questions as, "What constitutes the truth, the Dharma, the logic, and the right kind of hermeneutics?" All this, of course, will be supported by the Buddha's enlightenment, his capture of the realization of the mind-base, namely, the mind delineated as *prajñāpāramitā* which is the essence of Buddhist philosophy.

Avalokiteśvara Bodhisattva

The opening lines of the *Heart Sūtra* state:[5]

Avalokita, the Bodhisattva, engaged in deep meditative discipline of prajñāpāramitā, *perceived clearly that the five aggregates of being* (pañca-skandhāḥ)

*are all empty and he vows to relieve (save) all from
the suffering states of existence.*

Next, the *Sūtra* relates the Bodhisattva's experience of *prajñā*-wisdom — the capture of the nature of the truth of existence. In merely twenty-five words, the passage focusses on the aspect of reality as such, as compared to the aspect of clear perception of reality. The philosophy of the 260-word *Sūtra* explains the nature of truth by shifting around the first twenty-five words in a variety of ways. It can be said that the concept of truth had been with us from old, but it was never given a precise definition. Various assertions, such as, "What exists exists" and "God is truth" are made, but, upon close examination, the former expresses an epistemological position and the latter an ontological one; yet, if God's existence cannot be demonstrated in the first place, its truth, too, becomes clouded and cannot be determined. Although truth is longed for by many, it is all too often considered to be something profound and left dangling. It should be, of course, the most basic question in philosophy, but the discipline has failed immensely to grapple with it, leaving it for the most part as an irresolvable question. In this condition, numerous ideas have been spawned to explain what it is, only to collect and become further sources of ideological confusion; on the other hand, since people do not cast much doubt over scientific and mathematical truths, Western philosophy since Kant has witnessed the inevitable confrontation brought on by the apparent congruence of scientific truths (principles) and philosophical truths.

The fact that a principle exists means that there is something of a determined structure at its very basis. For example, the fact that something exists as seen through a microscope means that there is a structure inherent in the use of the microscope. Or, the fact that there is something up in the heavenly skies means that there is a structure to the telescope focussed in place that points at a satellite.

In the ontological situation in Western philosophy, however, neither the microscope nor telescope is taken into consideration. Moreover, the assertion, "God is truth," is made without probing into its demonstrative nature. Now, there is a trend in Japan to regard Western philosophy as pure philosophy and a rage to translate Western philosophical works as being vital activity of philosophers. But up to this day, I know of no one who could attest to the assertion that Westesrn philosophy is the truth or even has the truth.

If man were to take the truth in terms of something existing, then it would most certainly mean that he understands that there is a principle involved which, in turn, suggests the presence of a structure in epistemology. This strucuture, in the *Heart Sūtra*, is referred to as the 'structure of the mind' and the depiction of reality, as well. The initial twenty-five words of the *Sūtra* expound on this reality, a sutra appreciated and respected by Buddhists simply because it expresses so lucidly the very nature of truth.

Further on Avalokiteśvara Bodhisattva

The *Heart Sūtra* is criticized by some for its unstructured nature. This is said in the context that normally all Buddhist texts, especially with respect to early basic sutras, have a simple format, such as, beginning with the words, "Thus have I heard . . . " and relating to the time, place, and occasion of the Buddha's discourse. By contrast, the *Heart Sūtra* immediately launches into a dialogue between Avalokiteśvara Bodhisattva and Śāriputra, one of the ten trusted disciples of the Buddha. I believe, however, that this uncommon feature makes the *Heart Sūtra* all the more unique and challenges us to probe its deep meaning.

Although the Bodhisattva is known in China and Japan as Kanzeon Bosatsu (Japanese reading), in Sanskrit it is Avalokitésvara. Generally speaking, Avalokita refers to perception and Iśvara to freedom or unbounded nature. It would seem to me at least that, since Hsüan-tsang regarded the *Heart Sūtra* as the quintessential sutra of Buddhism which expounds on the Dharma, he took pains to keep the spirit of the original Sanskrit intact and rendered the Bodhisattva as Kanjizai (One who has perfect freedom of perception). Regardless of the propriety of the above interpretation, it can be said to depict the Dharmakāya Bodhisattva who exhibits, as it is, the structure of the mind-base in a triangular mode.

In accordance with my synthesis of various philosophies and the diagramming of the structure of the mind, it would seem that the three features of perception (*kan*), self (*ji*), and existence (*zai*), depicting Kanjizai Bodhisattva, form the points of a triangle and would correspond nicely with the subject (*ji*), object (*zai*) and synthesis (*kan*). When the left and right lobes of the brains are coupled in terms of the above triangular modes, the linkage occurs exactly at the foci (points) of the two triangles. This is known in Buddhism as the five aggregates of being (*skandhas*) which, inscribed as a large circle, had already been depicted in a diagram showing the emptiness of all elements of being. This is truly the structure of the mind and the true nature of the various *dharmas*.

The true nature of the mind is extremely difficult to delineate by merely utilizing such statements as "all aggregates of being are empty" and "the free unbounded nature of perception," just as a proverb aptly put the difficulty thus: "speech does not reach the eyes nor sound extend to the eyes." However, the diagram of the mind-base I drew earlier conforms to the truth dealt with in the *Heart Sūtra*. Accordingly, I believe the first twenty-five words of the *Heart Sūtra* truly express the realization of the mind-base and impress me greatly as a profound insight of the East. The structure of the free unbounded nature of perception is later on associated with the now familiar "One Mind, Two Aspects and Three Greatnesses" expounded in the *Awakening of Faith in the Mahāyāna*. As you will recall, I have rephrased the diagram of the mind-base as "One Mind, Two Aspects and Three Perceptions" for the sake of elucidating a methodology.

On Emptiness (*Śūnyatā*)

The discussion may have deviated into the subject of structure, but it should be emphasized that the single most important term in the *Heart Sūtra* is emptiness whose deep meanings are incalculable. As already shown in the diagram of the intuitive unconscious, the Buddhist concept of *mu* (nothingness) is a part of the realization of the mind-base and does not refer to nonbeing as against being, which are contraries, and results from mere conceptual analysis.

A well-known Japanese mathematician of the Meiji period, Yōichi Yoshida, asserts that the zero concept was discovered in India prior to the sixth century A.D. It was utilized in Arabia where algebra and logarithm developed and arrived in Europe in the thirteenth century A.D. to further develop mathematics as we know it today. Although it is acknowledged and emphasized that the zero simplified calculation and recording processes, replacing the abacus, there are little, if any, allusions to the value and strength of the zero in an equation as depicting the foundation of mathematical thinking. My personal feelings on the matter is that the discovery of the zero-concept in mathematics is not simply a shift in the calculation process from the abacus but that a deeper meaning lies in the fact that, philosophically, the equation expresses man's fundamental mode of thinking, i.e., it reveals, as it is, the nature of the structure of the mind-base. Accordingly, $1 + 2 = 3$ is a form of a dialectic, a logic, but far more important than this is the reflection on $(1 + 2) - 3 = 0$ which is another unique equation. Put another way, the zero-concept does not simply refer to nullity or nothingness but, most significantly, because of it, everything is possible and, contrarily, if it were not present nothing would materialize. Thus, it is extremely important to recognize this realizaton of the mind-base.

The words of the Bible that God created the world *ex nihilo* will not be accepted by those who are not religious, but, curiously enough, they are easily accommodated from the standpoint of the realization of the mind-base. This is asserted not in the ordinary sense of the meaning of creating the world out of mere nothingness. On this matter, I feel strongly that the realization of the mind-base, namely, that which is also the true essence of things expressed in the *Heart Sūtra*, is a great philosophic insight into the nature of things. That is, in the structure of the mind-base there is already nacent a structure that accommodates the realm of *mu* (emptiness). Incidentally, philosophers up to now have not really been aware of this important factor of the mind and have, instead, entertained in the linguistic and absolute sense the opposition between being and nonbeing. As stated earlier, the intuitive unconscious is involved with the realm of emptiness in a unique way and has nothing to do with mere conceptual understanding of nothingness or nonbeing.

Instructions to Śāriputra

The *Heart Sūtra* almost immediately has Avalokiteśvara Bodhisattva expound the supreme truth to Śāriputra thus:[6]

Form or corporeality (rūpa) *is not different from
emptiness (*śūnyatā*);
Emptiness is not different from form.
Form is at once emptiness;
Emptiness is at once form.
Feelings (*vedanā*), perceptual images* (samjñā),
imagery activities (samskāra) *and consciousness*
(vijñāna) *are, respectively, of the same nature
(i.e., emptiness)*

Previously, I had thought that the relatively short *Heart Sūtra* could be easily digested within a week. I was grossly mistaken. Coming across the above passage, which expresses the essence of the sutra, I was not only astounded but at wit's end. The reason for this is that the passage is identical to what has already been discussed as the emptiness of the five aggregates of being. The content is the same, except that now it is expressed in logical terms. In such a short treatise, how could it afford to repeat the same thought twice over? I researched ravenously in the various literatures for an answer, and, like Immanuel Kant, I had to do some philosophizing even though I was in no mood to do so. Then, subsequently, I realized suddenly that the Buddha's philosophy (his teachings) began here with the distinction between reality as such (*jissō*) and clear perception (*kanshō*) of that reality. If considered within the context of this revelation, the assertion, "Form is at once emptiness," contains all the explanations to the philosophical questions that have been raised one after another, such as, questions on epistemology and ontology, truth, solutions to universal disputations, Zeno's paradoxes, ideological questions, and those dealing with the definitions on the nature of man and of philosophy itself. All these questions and many more were, in short, resolved in the single statement, "the five aggregates of being are empty," which is just another expression for the nature of the realization of the mind-base.

I realized, however, how difficult it is to philosophize by merely analyzing literary sources. In consequence, since the exposition of the *Heart Sūtra* should not merely serve philosophers and religionists but, instead, should aim individual readers toward philosophizing on their own, I have felt the need to help them along to derive a proper understanding by expressing in terms of symbols and metaphors, such as the use of equations and diagrams, to map out the stages in the methodology. The use of metaphors and diagrams, seen from the historical controversy between rationalism and empiricism, makes one realize the urgency to employ them. The situation, incidentally, gives us a good reason to understand the use of numerous metaphors in Indian logic proper. Since language is conventional (a type of symbolism) and the listener interprets it in accordance with his own condition of the mind-base, I realized suddenly why the *Heart Sutra* was apprehensive of the possibility of going astray, and, a fortiori, distinguished between true reality as such and its clear perception which is to be realized in meditative discipline.

Returning to the above quoted passage, "Form is not different from emptiness and emptiness is not different from form. Form is at once emptiness and emptiness is at once form," a similar structure is found in early Buddhism thus:[7]

> This being, that comes to be; from the arising of this, that arises; this not being, that ceases; from the ceasing of this, that ceases.

It is the familiar formula for the doctrine of interrelational origination, a doctrine which presents a continuity in the whole Buddhist tradition and becomes the basis for the unique characteristic of the Mahāyāna dialectic of emptiness. Incidentally, a type of dialectical logic is seen in the so-called Indian *tetralemma* where the four possible ways of asserting anything are posted, i.e., is, is not, both is and is not, and neither is nor is not. The second century Buddhist, Nāgārjuna, utilized them in criticizing his opponent's views.[8]

In Western logical thinking, the mode of thesis, antithesis, and synthesis is generally classified as a kind of dialectic, but, based on the Buddhist realization of the mind-base, a dialectic is not so easily formulated and, rather than the logical nature, the importance ought to be placed on what the logical form itself essentially signifies. If this realization of the mind-base were to be ignored, the dialectic would not be able to function as a dialectic should. On the contrary, were the realization of the mind-base to become the foundation of a dialectic, despite the formal nature, even such thoroughgoing negative logic (*prasaṅga*) employed by Madhyamaka philosophy would be able to adequately function as critical analysis and clarification of ideas. Thus, it is inaccurate to say that since Eastern logic did not develop, it does not have an explanation for the attainment of the realization of the mind-base. Moreover, it is extremely difficult to determine which side, East or West, is more rational in dealing with the logic of things. Even if a formal refutation were to be carried out, without being completely convinced in the true sense, there would still be some problems with regards to proving that formal logic is the only form of rational and advanced logic in the world.

The motive force that propelled modern science to new heights is undoubtedly mathematics. Perhaps it was Spinoza who said, in effect, that even God finds it difficult to deny that $1 + 2 = 3$. In regard to its history of development, even in mathematics, long regarded as a form of truth, many fundamental problems have arisen since the discovery of set theory to cause mathematicians and philosophers to question the very nature or foundations of mathematics.

It would seem to me that there is a basic difference between formal logic and dialectical logic based on the realization of the mind-base.

The analysis may have deviated somewhat, but it was simply to reiterate the fact that there is a vast difference between the emptiness realized in *prajña*-intuition as expounded in the *Heart Sūtra* and our ordinary conception of nonbeing as opposed to being. This was clearly brought out in the *Sūtra* thus: "Corporeality (form) is emptiness. This is the same with feelings, imagery, activity of imagery and consciouness." The exposition of emptiness realized in *prajña*-intuition is the aim of *prajñā* philosophy and veritably the essence of the *Heart Sūtra*.

In a word, the gist of "Form or corporeality is not different from emptiness, and so on" is that they represent the epistemology of Buddhist philosophy and, at the same time, express the standpoint of that epistemology based on the realization of the mind-base. More specifically, it means that without form, there would be no epistemic function of feelings, imagery, and so forth. And vice versa, without the epistemic function of feelings, imagery, and so forth, there would be no form.

The above analysis could easily be expressed in the form of a mathematical equation. For example, the equation $1 + 2 = 3$ takes on at least the form of Western dialectic in the nature of thesis-antithesis-synthesis and is accepted as a mathematical truth. On the other hand, when the same equation is tranformed into the following, $(1 + 2) - 3 = 0$, a unique dialectic is seen, as expressed in the *Heart Sūtra* thus: "Form or corporeality is not different from emptiness, emptiness is not different from form: and so on." In this situation, the zero (0) is never meant as a nonbeing (i.e., literal nothingness). In other words, the emptiness of *prajñā*-intuition and the discovery of the mathematical zero concur in that they are founded on the realization of the mind-base and not on the dichotomous opposition between being and nonbeing.

When all this is considered in light of epistemology, can we say that the mathematical equation $1 + 2 = 3$ is a form of an ontology or epistemology? Or, is it something in the nature of what had already been analyzed as the essentials of the *Heart Sūtra*? No one could come up with a definite answer. If the problem were posed differently, for example, by considering form or corporeality (*rūpa*) as an existent and consciousness (*vijñāna*) as awareness, with man's cognitive process comparable to the TV set, then what could we say about the whole apparatus of reception? Is it a matter of ontology, epistemology, or conceptualism? Such fundamental questions would arise even when the apparatus is not emitting anything materialistic or corporeal.

Nature of the Various *Dharmas*

In the *Heart Sūtra*, Avalokiteśvara Bodhisattva goes on to explain:[9]

> *Oh, Śāriputra: Here these various* dharmas *have empty characteristics. There is neither origination nor destruction; neither purity nor impurity; neither increase nor decrease.*

The above so-called six negations are somewhat comparable to the eight negations (Eight-Noes) of Nāgārjuna as seen in his dedicatory verse of *Mūlamadhyamakakārikā*. Piṅgala, one of the commentators of Nāgārjuna's work, utilizes the negations to expound on the supreme truth of things (*paramārtha-sat*) , and Asaṅga, the Yogācārin (i.e., adherent of the consciousness-only doctrine) also recognizes their values as a vital component of Madhyamaka thought. All these, then, substantiate the importance attached to the meaning of the verse found in *prajñāpāramitā* thought. In consequence, I have interpreted this important verse from the standpoint of true reality and clear perception derived from meditative insight and have concluded that it fired the development of later doctrines, such as, the true nature (*tathatā*) of *dharmas* as expounded in the *Awakening of Faith in the Mahāyāna*. It is also linked to the concept of emptiness of all *skandhas*, the central issue of the *Heart Sūtra*, and equatable to the realization of the mind-base. All of this is seen to be another instance of perceiving the mind-base from the standpont of the true *dharmic* nature which is man's true consciousness (*satori*) depicted in the form of a mirror metaphor.

I would like to emphasize that careful attention be paid to the word "here" (*iha* in Sanskrit) which precedes "these various *dharmas* have empty characteristics." For I firmly believe that the whole assertion describes the inner content of enlightenment of Avalokiteśvara Bodhisattva expressed in the single term, emptiness, with respect to all five *skandhas*. On the basis of this, I have introduced a series of diagrams which describe a type of 'philosophy of depth-*prajñā*,' if you will. I also feel that mere comparison of this philosophy of depth-*prajñā* with the literal meaning of *prajñā* does not allow one to perceive the real sense of the thought in the *Heart Sūtra*. Some may assert that the concept of interrelational origination by thusness (*shinnyo engi*) came after the *Heart Sūtra*. My response is that the Buddhist Dharma stems from the Buddha's original enlightenment (Dharma = Truth of Existence) and that any subsequent development of ideas, such as, the various doctrines on interrelational origination, are nothing but seeds germinating from the Buddha's enlightenment. Accordingly, it is not in error to utilize the concept of true *dharmic* nature (*tathatā*) to interpret subsequently established Buddhist texts and their contents. If, for instance, these texts do not expound on the depth-*prajñā* of the *Heart Sūtra* but on some other questions relative to the mind, then for whose mental function and purpose are these six negations or eight negations? Thus, I have interpreted the true *dharmic* nature in modern language as a dimension (*jigen*) of being. Whether or not the true *dharmic* nature is the same as the dimension of being will undoubtedly be a crucial question in the future. If something other than the dimension of being is discovered to add to the interpretative effort, then philosophic endeavor would progress that much more and be enriched thereby. For my part, I am satisfied now to interpret it as a dimension of being, in order to bring focus on a single diagram depicting the emptiness of the five *skandhas*, so that we may have a clear perception of what I may call the interrelational origination by the perception of emptiness or by other doctrines, such as, interrelational origination by thusness (*tathatā*) or by storehouse consciousness (*ālaya-vijñāna*), that range from early Buddhism to the Mahāyāna. I further believe that with the interpretation of the dimension of being expressed diagrammatically, a host of problems arising in the historical context in Western philosophy, such as, the medieval universal disputations or Zeno's paradoxes, will be clarified. Moreover, there will be the possibility of comparing Eastern psychology with Western psychoanalysis.

Although the discussion may have digressed, the interpretation of the six negations is quite clear. It reflects the Avalokiteśvara Bodhisattva's capture of the identity of the realization of the mind-base and the emptiness of the five *skandhas*. Thus, all *skandhas* are nonoriginating and nondestructing, nonpure and nonimpure, and nonincreasing and nondecreasing. The identity is conversive with both inner and outer realms and also applicable to man's inner and outer being, i.e., relative to the realm of epistemology, as well as to ontological principles. In such a way, it defines the coexistent nature of man and the universe in the total turning of the wheel of existence (*saṃsāra*).

Present day Western philosophy by and large still treats existents within the spatio-temporal context and that seems to generate the fundamental problem of interpreting them. But how could we, for example, accommodate plane geometry, which does not function within the spatio-temporal context? The thought of placing existents merely within the spatio-temporal context is indeed in the realm of conventionality, but instead, if they were accommodated within the total dimension of being, it would be possible to have discourse on not only the spatio-temporal context but also on the

concept of infinity (infinite dimension) that occurs in both plane
geometry and philosophy proper.

Nature of Emptiness (*Śūnyatā*)

The *Heart Sūtra* goes on to say:[10]

> *In emptiness, therefore, there are no form or corporeality,*
> *feeling, imagery, activity of imagery and consciousness.*
>   *(reference to the five* skandhas*)*
> *There are no eyes, ears, nose, tongue, body and mind.*
>   *(reference to the six sense faculties)*
> *There are no sight, sound, smell, taste, tactility*
> *and mental object (*dharma*).*
>   *(reference to the six sense objects; the*
>   *faculties and objects refer to the twelve sense*
>   *realms, twelve* āyatanas*)*
> *There are no sense faculties, sense objects and mental*
> *objects (reference to the eighteen* dharmic *realms,*
>   *eighteen* dhātus*)*

The above has relevance to the pet formula mentioned earlier,
i.e., "this being, that comes to be; from the arising of this, that
arises, and so on." As there is no corporeality in emptiness, the rest
of the *skandhas, āyatanas,* and *dhātus* are also bereft of any existent nature or objective status (*svabhāva*), thus expressing in clear
terms the doctrine of interrelational origination. Therein everything is in relationship of mutual dependence and mutual contrast,
that without one the other will not manifest. When stated in the
above fashion, the immediate reaction might be that it is only
natural that such is the case and that one need not probe the philosophy of *prajñāpāramitā* to know it. But here again, it cannot be
emphasized too much that the concept of emptiness harbors no
contraries and has nothing to do with the ordinary understanding
of being and nonbeing.

To expand, in the diagram of the mind-base, it was stated that
emptiness in *prajñā*-intuition is the "true emptiness of wondrous

being" and that the identity of the structure of emptiness and the dimension of zero is already a fact in the realization of the mind-base. By contrast, the ordinary understanding of being and non-being is merely in reference to phenomenal constructs; thus, there is a vast difference in terms of consciousness. This is clearly seen by examining the diagram of the mind-base expressed as a dimension of being. In the emptiness of *prajñā*-intuition and the zero in mathematics, there is an antinomical self-identity of the point and infinity because the dimensional realm includes two mutually opposing dimensions, i.e., one signifying the unifying (integrative) point and the other the ever-expanding infinity. This may be a difficult theory to comprehend, but under no circumstances should it be confused with the common understanding of nonbeing (nothingness) based on the two dimensional opposition of being and nonbeing. An illustration or example may be in order here.

Let us return to Demonstration 1-2, coordinate axis, presented on page 32. When two coordinates are written on a single sheet of paper, the intersection of the two (X, Y) becomes a point. As this point becomes the reference for the determination of units, such as, 1, 2, 3, 4, and so on, the initial point and the sheet surface which has the nature of infinite expansion would both constitute a zero or emptiness. Common sense will normally lead us to consider the zero and emptiness as simply nothing, but it should be noted that the number one is not possible without the zero, nor the two without a one, and so forth.

Let us pursue the matter further in the context of the Buddha's enlightenment. It is allegedly said that he at age 35, on Dec. the 8th, attained enlightenment just as the morning star shone brilliantly. Now, the interpretation of the morning star is crucial. It should not be simply a shining entity but rather a star seen in fullness analogous to seeing Rubin's sketch (Demonstration 1-1, p. 30), for there is prominently present the nature of emptiness in respect to the total heavenly emptiness. It was not the case of a mere existent shining star but a brilliant star within the total firmament. The Buddha, it would seem, had at that instant realized the so-called *prajñā*-emptiness. The above are, of course, my personal inferences. But normally everyone does experience the illusions presented in Rubin's sketch, and everyone knows that a picture without a background is not a picture, nor a photo without contours a photo. But actually to refer to Rubin's sketch or to the

Buddha's enlightenment is for the first time to become aware of the meaning attached to the discovery of a principle. That is to say, although normally the concept of emptiness would end by being accommodated in the realm of the intuitive unconsciousness, since it was realized by the Buddha it paved the way for a huge development as a Buddhist principle and, in particular, as *prajñā*-emptiness.

We all know that we are alive at the moment. But are we conscious of the fact that we are alive in the eternal present? Are we cognizant of the fact that each person has it within himself to live or not to live his life fully in accordance with the rise or nonrise of the supreme present moment? If that be the case, then *prajñā*-emptiness and the zero will relate respectively to the zero dimension (of life) and the absolute in terms of antinomical self-identity. Similarly, time and temporal spread and plane surface and volume will relate respectively to the nature of antinomical self-identity. Brought within such conditions, I believe, most of the baffling philosophical problems would be resolved.

Nature of Ignorance (*Avidyā*)

The Heart *Sūtra* concludes the analysis:[11]

> *No ignorance nor the destruction of ignorance . . .*
> *No old age-death nor the destruction of old age-death.*
> *No suffering nor the rise of suffering; no cessation*
> *of suffering nor the way out of suffering.*
> *No knowledge nor the grasping for it since nothing is*
> *grasped.*

The above, needless to say, has implications of the doctrine of twelvefold interrelational origination and the fourfold Noble Truth. It is alleged that the Buddha perceived them both positively (*anuloma*) and negatively (*paṭiloma*) and enjoyed the bliss of the Dharma (the truth of existence). Being a Buddhist principle of being, this passage is quite important, and yet, oddly enough, beginning with the Abhidharma period, it began to be interpreted in embryological terms. And later on, even in the Mahāyāna tradition, no adequate and convincing explanation is found. As the twelvefold nature of the interrelational origination is rendered in diverse ways it only shows the difficulty of its interpretation. I even inquired into Nāgārjuna's *Mūlamadhyamakakārikā*, especially Chapter 26 on the Examination of Twelve-fold Nature, but it, too, failed to provide an adequate analysis by following the Theravāda interpretation in the main. Generally speaking, then, there is no consistent interpretation of the doctrine.

In my search through Buddhist commentary works, I noted that a confusion had occurred in the treatment of the twelvefold nature of interrelational origination and the causal nature of Buddhist dialectic. I was, however, heartened to see that the *Treatise on Twelve Gates* (*Jūnimon-ron*)[12] of Nāgārjuna clearly distinguishes between the two natures. For example, the first chapter on the examination of causal nature asserts thus:[13]

> There are two aspects of causal nature in the arising of factors of experience (*dharmas*), one internal and the other external. Likewise, there are two aspects of causal conditions (*pratyayas*), one internal and the other external. The external causal nature can be likened to the production of a pot, i.e., the harmonious combination of such matters as the clay, potting wheel and potter . . . The internal causal conditions refer namely to the twelvefold ignorance (*avidyā*), vital activity (*samskāra*), consciousness (*vijñāna*), subjective-objective forms (*nāma-rūpa*), six sense faculties (*salāyatana*), contact (*sparśa*) feeling (*vedanā*), desire (*tṛṣṇā*), attachment (*upādāna*), formation of being (*bhava*), birth (*jāti*), and old age-death (*jarāmaraṇa*), where each preceding condition becomes the basis for the rise of the succeeding one.

As I was unable to come through with a proper explanation, due to the rather nebulous accounting of the causal nature of things, I would like to advance my own theory. It would seem to me, first of all, that the twelvefold nature was primarily a systematic treatment of man's suffering, karma, and delusory nature based on the fundamental ignorance (*avidyā*) of human course of events. A diagrammatic presentation would be as follows:

Ignorance

karma
(vital activity)   suffering

desire   attachment,
                                formation of being

birth   old age-death

The diagram depicts both a temporal continuity in the nature of
a dialectic (right side) and a linkage of time and space (left side).
Each segment includes suffering, karma, and delusory nature
which are covered by the umbrella of ignorance. Since it would be
cumbersome and wordy to designate the workings of ignorance in
each and every segment, it was acknowledged that ignorance appears only at the beginning of the causal chain and that the
number of links increased or decreased with later interpretations.
Accordingly, the links were discussed in terms of twelvefoldness or
tenfoldness or any other number of links. And as each link is
covered by ignorance (inclusive of suffering, karma, and
delusion), then it would be possible to interpret the doctrine of interrelational origination either symmetrically (*anuloma*; clockwise)
or asymmetrically (*paṭiloma*; counterclockwise) and thus retain the
character of continuity in terms of a single principle. It would be
difficult now to analyze and determine the increase or decrease in
the number of links or the modification of the doctrine as com-

pared with the Buddha's time, but it would not be unreasonable to infer that there was the consistent and continuous reference to suffering, karma, and delusion.

The scheme of the twelvefold interrelational origination is based on (initiated by) ignorance, depicting the process of falling into suffering states of existence, but the opposite direction (asymmetric) is the way to liberation described in the famous fourfold Noble Truth. The four aspects of the truth are the universal nature of suffering, the rise of suffering states, the cessation of suffering, and the way out of suffering—all of which is modelled after the order of treatment by the doctor. To wit, in medical practice, the first requirement is to properly diagnose the illness of the patient, the nature of suffering. Next, it is necesary to derive a correct pathology of the illness, hence the cause of the illness. Then the proper treatment is administered which is comparable to the cessation of suffering. Finally, the restoration to a normal healthy being is the way out of suffering, which is further prescribed by following the eightfold Noble Path, i.e., right view, right thought, right speech, right action, right livelihood, right endeavor, right mindfulness, and right concentration.

The *Heart Sūtra* abbreviates the analysis of the twelvefold interrelational origination by listing only the first and last segments and assumes the same treatment for the rest of the segments. Man is presumed healthy in his original state of being (i.e., Buddhist reference to the fact that all sentient beings are endowed with the Buddha-nature) and which also means that the twelvefold interrelational origination is unnecessary (i.e., if necessary then reference to Buddhist ignorance = suffering). Yet, suffering or illness never seems to end in this world, for without it there would be no necessity for the Fourfold Noble Truth and likewise for medical practice. The fact of the matter is that illness continues to occur, and thus the medical profession thrives. Moreover, the fact that a healthy being falls into illness and later recovers does not mean that he has become the wise for it, nor that he has gained any merits by it because there is "no knowledge nor the grasping for it since nothing is grasped."

Man should, therefore, always from the outset attempt to intimate with his own realization of the mind-base (= the nature of true man). But, since he normally does not, he falls into the 'illness' of identifying the mind or the self with the elements of the intuitive unconscious. Thus, the healthy state as the original condition of man does not lend itself to any gain of merits or to an increase of knowledge. The Zen pithy remark is cogent: "this mind is the very nature of the Buddha; the mind at once is the Buddha." Furthermore, the following assertion is recalled:[14]

> The Buddhas and Tathāgatas are the embodiment of *dharmadhātu* (the realm of the *dharmas*, i.e., reality as such). They always enter into the minds and thoughts of all sentient creatures. In consequence, when you are mindful of the Buddha, the mind is at once the manifestation of his thirty-two auspicious major physical features and eighty minor features. The mind creates the Buddha; indeed the mind is the Buddha.

Thus our ordinary minds, as they are, have all the potential of activating the supreme nature from within the intuitive unconscious, the initial and fundamental ground from which the enlightened realm of existence is realized.

Since the remaining part of the *Heart Sūtra* enters into strictly religious matters and aspirations, I shall omit it and end the comparative analysis of the sutra in the context of the various disciplines.

(This ends the major portion of The Logic of Unity. *The author has taken a long path in the analysis of the logic of unity, but, hopefully, the problematic areas have been sufficiently aired and somewhat cleared and some bridges of understanding built for the intercourse between Eastern and Western ways of thinking. It is hoped that his contributions will provoke serious reactions and responses in ways that would further probe into the basic epistemic nature of man and that eventually the unwarranted schism between the scientific and humanistic sciences would be resolved. — Trans.)*

Postscript

The present work is far from being the result of strict academic research, for it is, as suggested here and there, to serve as a foundation stone for a philosophy that truly comes to grips with the problems of man and society, indeed, a point of departure for learning how to philosophize. Accordingly, there is no attempt to resolve in any ultimate sense the various problems that arise in the world. Rather, it is to give meaningful direction to the understanding of the rise of such problems and thereby contribute as much as possible toward a purposeful accommodation. The discussion in part has been rambling, if not repetitive, on familiar themes, but it was so only to emphasize the crucial points relative to human nature, consciousness, and endeavor.

I do not for a moment entertain any thought that the present work has arrived at or is on the verge of arriving at the absolute nature of things. On the contrary, I would feel greatly vindicated should the work provoke the reader to seriously engage in relevant discussions and inspire him or her to develop the zeal and taste for philosophical methodology and understanding.

Hōsaku Matsuo

Notes

Translator's Introduction

1. For a good overview of the Kyoto School, see Thomas P. Kasulis, "The Kyoto School and the West: Review and Evaluation," *The Eastern Buddhist*, XV, 2 (August 1982), 125–144. See also Frederick Franck, ed., *The Buddha Eye: An Anthology of the Kyoto School* (New York: Crossroad Publishing Co., 1982). Other helpful works by followers of Nishida philosophy are: Keiji Nishitani, *Religion and Nothingness* (Berkeley: University of California Press, 1982), tr. by Jan Van Bragt; Yoshinori Takeuchi, *The Heart of Buddhism* (New York: Crossroad Publishing Co., 1983), tr. by James W. Heisig; Masao Abe, *Zen and Western Thought* (Honolulu: University of Hawaii Press, 1985), ed. William R. LaFleur.

2. Kitarō Nishida, *A Study of Good* (Japan: Ministry of Education Publication, 1960), tr. by V.H. Viglielmo. Incidentally, *From the Acting to the Seeing* (*Hatarakumono-kara-miru-mono-e* 働くもの から見るものへ) has yet to be translated into English.

3. See the excerpts of "The Problem of Japanese Culture" (Nihon-bunka-no-mondai), translated by Masao Abe in the *Sources of Japanese Tradition*, compiled by Ryūsaku Tsunoda, Wm. Theodore de Bary & Donald Keene (New York: Columbia University Press, 1958), pp. 857–872. Nishida was criticized by the ultranationalist elements for his forays into a synthesis of East-West thought.

4. Op. cit., *A Study of Good*, p. v.

127

5. It is interesting to note that his postretirement work, *Fundamental Problems of Philosophy* (*Tetsugaku-no-konpon-mondai* 哲学の根本問題) (Tokyo: Sophia University, 1970), tr. by David A. Dilworth, p. 32, Nishida, for example, clearly makes a Kegon statement: "The most concrete true reality is the actual world of present actuality in which individuals mutually determine one another."

Preface

1. Hōsaku Matsuo, editor and contributor, *Hikaku-tetsugaku-hōhōron-no-kenkyū* 比較哲学方法論の研究 (*Studies in the Methodology of Comparative Philosophy* (Tokyo: Tokyo Shoseki, 1980).

2. Karl Jaspers, *Way to Wisdom: An Introduction to Philosophy* (*Einführung in die Philosophie*), tr. by Ralph Manheim (London: Victor Gollancz Ltd., 1951), p. 28.

3. Ibid. pp. 29–30.

4. This is an abbreviated form of the famous passage on 'emptiness' (*śūnyatā*) found in the *Heart Sūtra* (*Prajñāpāramitāhṛdaya-sūtra*). Confer, for example, Edward Conze, *Buddhist Wisdom Books* (London: George Allen & Unwin Ltd., 1958), pp. 77–107, for an in-depth analysis of the concept.

5. *Hannya-kū* 般若空 ('prajñā-emptiness') is a special term, a neologism, derived from the early Mahāyāna works known as the *Prajñāpāramitā Sūtras* (*Sūtras on the Perfection of Wisdom*). These sutras expound on the practice of the way of the Bodhisattva who perceives everything under the aegis of 'emptiness' which is the result of his training in the perfections of being (*pāramitās*), thus, the hyphenated term.

6. This saying is only a portion of the stock sayings casually attributed to the Zen patriarch, Bodhidharma. Other related sayings are: "Transmission from one mind to another"; "special transmission apart from the textual teachings," "Inexpressible in words or letters"; and "This very mind is the Buddha."

Chapter I

1. Translation is from the Chinese sources. *Kuan-wu-liang-shou-fu-ching* 觀無量壽佛經 (*Taishō Edition of the Tripitaka*; Vol. 12, No. 365, 343a). The English translation was done by Junjirō Takakusu in *The Sacred Books of the East*, XLIX. *The Amitayur-dhyāna-sūtra*; p. 178. (Delhi: Motilal Banarsidass, 1965 reprint.)

2. As it will be discussed in detail later, the *A wakening of Faith in the Mahāyāna, Ta-ch'eng-ch'i-hsin-lun* 大乘起信論 (*Taishō* Edition of the Tripitaka; Vol. 32, no. 1666) presents the famous doctrines of One-Mind, Two Aspects and Three Greatnesses. In the second section on the Establishment of the Doctrine, it expounds the basic thought in the following way: "In expounding the Mahāyāna in general there are two types. What are the two? They are first the Dharma and second the Doctrine." In short, the truth of Mahāyāna Buddhism is the Dharma, and the exposition of its superiority is the Doctrine. The Dharma refers to the totality of *dharmas* encompassing the worldly and otherworldly realms of existence, i.e., the minds of all sentient beings. These minds of sentient beings, endowed with the illimitable and immeasurable Buddha-nature (*buddhatā*), point at the supreme *One Mind* which is expressive of the substance of the Mahāyāna. It is referred to as the Aspect of the Mind in Thusness (*tathatā*). On the other hand, it is also known as the Aspect of the Mind in *saṃsāra* due to the ordinary mind's *saṃsāric* changes in the process of interrelational origination. These two comprise the Two Aspects.

The Aspect of the Mind in *Saṃsāra* is instituted by the Three Greatnesses, namely, the Greatness of Substance, of Form (or Attribute), and of Function. The Greatness of Substance manifests the thusness (*tathatā*) of the mind, in particular in reference to the unchanging characteristics of the process of *saṃsāric* changes. The Greatness of Form refers to the manifestation of thusness in its special character and potentiality, corresponding to the Buddha's wisdom and compassion. It also refers to the Womb of Thuscome (*tathāgatagarbha*) wherein all sentient beings are received in it, and, vice versa, all sentient beings potentially possess it. The Greatness of Function is the work of the Thuscome (*tathāgata*) and refers to the meritable power of bringing forth goodness in all worldly and otherworldly beings. In such a way, the fundamental doctrine of Mahāyāna Buddhism is revealed by way of the doctrines of One Mind, Two Aspects and Three Greatnesses. (For an Englsh translation of the relevant passages, see Yoshito Hakeda, *The Awakening of Faith Attributed to Aśvaghosha* (New York: Columbia University Press, 1967), pp. 28–52.

3. Consult Note 2. Profound discussion was always generated as the seminar group read the *Awakening of Faith in the Mahāyāna.*

4. To sum up, I would like to present the following additional diagrams:

(1) (undifferentiated) (nondiscriminative knowledge)

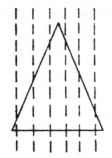

realm of intuition and unconsciousness where the subject, object and synthesis are indistinguishable

(2) (differentiated) (discriminative knowledg)

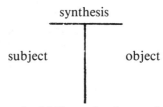

ignorance (*avidyā*) results due to the separation into the three elements

(3) (realization)

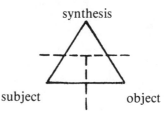

One Mind or Unity is realized due to the integration of the three elements

5. For a detailed discussion on the matter of ignorance, see Yoshito Hakeda, *The Awakening of Faith Attributed to Aśvaghosha*; op. cit., pp. 43–53.

6. Friedrich Engels, *Ludwig Feuerbach and the Outcomes of Classical German Philosophy* (New York: International Publishers, 1941), p. 20.

7. F.S.C. Northrop, *The Meeting of East and West: An Inquiry Concerning World Understanding* (New York: The MacMillan Company, 1946).

8. Nakamura Hajime, *Hikaku-shisō-ron* 比較思想論 (*Treatise on Comparativew Thought*) (Tokyo: Iwanami Soten, 1960), pp. 163f.

9. Nāgārjuna, *Mūlamadhyamakakārikā* (Verses on the Fundamental Middle Doctrine), XXIV, 8, 9.

10. Watsuji Tetsurō, *Ethics as the Study of Man* (Tokyo: Iwanami Shoten, 1962).

11. A proposal made in response to a seminar on "What is Democracy?" and conducted in the Seminar in Social Education, Kanazawa University, Japan. It was subsequently published in the *Kanazawa University Social Education Quarterly*, No. 38, September, 1972.

Chapter II

1. Friedrich Engels, *Ludwig Feuerbach and the Outcome of Classical German Philosophy* (New York: International Publishers, 1941), pp. 20–21.

2. *Lesser Discourses to Mālunkyā (putta)*, Sutta 63, *Majjhimanikāya*, English translation by I. B. Horner, *The Collection of the Middle Length Sayings*, Vol. II, (London: Luzac & Company, Ltd., 1957 reprint), pp. 97–101.

3.   Variously translated as "sameness equals difference or discrimination," "equality is at once discrimination," or "the undifferentiated realm is at once the differentiated." This paradoxical nature of 'equation' (qua) is the fountainhead of Buddhist thought which will be expanded in Mahāyāna Buddhism and becomes the basis for the practical application of Buddhist principles as witnessed in the influence on the various Far Eastern cultural and performing arts.

4.   In Pali, *Mahāparinibbāna-suttanta* (*The Book of the Great Decease*), tr. by T. W. Rhys Davids. For a selection, see E. A. Burtt, ed., "Buddha's Farewell Address," *The Teachings of the Compassionate Buddha*, Part I, 6, (New York: New American Library, Inc., 1981 reprint), pp. 47-50.

5.   The ten profound gates actually refer to the way experiential events arise or how interrelational origination manifests in each moment of experience. They were expounded by Chih-yen (602–668 A.D.), the second patriarch of Hua-yen (Kegon) School. The latest translation is by Thomas Cleary, "Ten Mysterious Gates of the Unitary Vehicle of the Hua-yen," in *Entry Into the Inconceivable* (Honolulu: University of Hawaii Press, 1983), pp. 125–146.

6.   The Eightfold Noble Path is part of the Fourfold Noble Truth, to wit, Universal Nature of Suffering, Rise of Suffering, Cessation of Suffering, and the Way Out of Suffering, the latter of which is constituted by the Eightfold Noble Path. For an abbreviated presentation of the Buddha's first discourse, see E. A. Burtt's *Teachings of the Compassionate Buddha*, op. cit. pp. 29–32.

7.   *Daihatsu-nehan-gyō*   大般涅槃經   (*Mahāparinirvāṇa Sūtra*). *Taishō Edition of the Tripitaka*, Vol. 12, No. 374, 501a–502b, 596a–b. This Chinese text is much longer and detailed in its exposition of the final days of the Buddha than its Pali text counterpart (see note 4).

8.   Ryūsaku Tsunoda, Wm. Theodore de Bary, Donald Keene, compiled, *Sources of Japanese Tradition* (New York: Columbia University Press, 1958), p. 52.

9.   This is in reference to the Buddhist doctrine of karma which, contrary to common knowledge, does not carry the meaning of determinism or necessitarianism. It actually depicts present action or deed that has certain effect later, and thus it is an important volitional act as graphically stated in the first verse of the *Dhammapada:*

All that we are is the result of what we have thought; it is founded on our thoughts, it is made up of our thoughts. If a man speaks or acts with an evil thought, pain follows him, as the wheel follows the foot of the ox that draws the carriage.

. . . . If a man speaks or acts with a pure thought, happiness follows him, like a shadow that never leaves him.

See E. A. Burtt, *Teachings of the Compassionate Buddha*, op cit., p. 52.

10.   Translated by F. Max Muller in *The Sacred Books of the East*, XLIX (Delhi: Motilal Banarsidass, 1965 reprint).

11.   Confer with the following texts: *Dīgha-nikāya* (*Dialogues of the Buddha*) 34; *Majjhima-nikāya (Middle Length Sayings)* 3, 6, 77; *Samyutta-nikāya* (*Kindred Sayings*) XV, 9; *Aṅguttara-nikāya* (*Gradual Sayings*) III, 99; V, 23. For a systematic discussion of the divine or supernormal powers, see K. N. Jayatilleke, *Early Buddhist Theory of Knowledge* (London: George Allen & Unwin, Ltd., 1963), pp. 437–39.

Chapter III

1.   ‟ *Ta-pan-jo-po-lo-mi-to-ching* (大般若波羅蜜多經), Chinese translation by Hsüan-tsang, 玄奘 Taishō Edition of the Tripitaka, Vols. 5–6. No. 220.

2.   In Chinese, more specifically, *K'ai-yuan-shih-chiao-lu* (開元釈 教録 in 20 fascicles compiled by Chih-sheng (智昇 668–740 A.D.) which is an exhaustive T'ang Dynasty catalogue of Buddhist works. *Taishō Edition of the Tripitaka*, Vol. 55, No. 2154.

3.   Christmas Humphreys, *Buddhism* (New York: Harper & Row, 1970), p. 11.

4.   Kitarō Nishida, *Zen-no-kenkyū,* 善の研究 tr. by V. H. Viglielmo, *A Study of Good* (A publication of the Japanese National Commission for Unesco, Ministry of Education, 1960), pp. 42–48.

5.   For a detailed analysis of the opening lines, see Edward Conze,

Buddhist Wisdom Books (The Diamond Sutra and The Heart Sutra) (London: George Allen & Unwin, Ltd., 1958), pp. 77–81.

6.   Ibid., see pp. 81–85, for further analysis of this most imporant assertion.

7.   This is the famous 'formula' for the interrelational origination found in various parts of the early Buddhist texts as, for example, in the *Samyutta-nikāya*, 12.4.37. Translated by Mrs. Rhys Davids and assisted by F. L. Woodward, *The Book of the Kindred Sayings*, Part II (London: Luzac & co., Ltd., 1952 reprint), p. 45.

8.   Nāgārjuna, *Mūlamadhyamakakārikā* (*Verses on the Fundamental Middle Doctrine*), I, Verse 1:

> Nowhere and at no time could entities ever exist by originating out of themselves, from others, from both (selves and others) and from lack of causes.

9.   See Edward Conze, op. cit., pp. 85–89, for an analysis of the six characteristics of 'empty' *dharmas*.

10.   Ibid., pp. 89–91 for further discussion of the subject matter.

11.   Ibid., pp. 91–92 for further analysis.

12.   *Treatise on Twelve Gates* (*Shih-erh-men-lun*) 十二門論 by Nāgārjuna. This work exists only in the Chinese. *Taishō Edition of the Tripitaka*, Vol. 30, No. 1568. For an English translation, see Hsueh-li Cheng, *Nāgārjuna's Twelve Gate Treatise* (Dordrecht: D. Reidel Publishing Company, 1982).

13.   Ibid., Chapter I (Kuan-in-yüan-men) 觀因緣門 *Taishō Edition*, Vol. 30, No. 1568, 159–160b. Hsueh-li Cheng, p. 55.

14.   Translated by Junjirō Takakusu in *The Sacred Books of the East*, XLIX (Delhi: Motilal Banarsidass, 1965 reprint). *The Amitayurdhyāna-sūtra*, p. 178. Translation is from the Chinese sources (*Taishō Edition of the Tripitaka*, Vol. 12, 343a).

Glossary of Terms

absolute truth; *shintai* (真諦); *paramārtha-satya*

action, deed, volitional act; *gō* (業); *karma*

all beings are endowed with *Buddha*-nature; *issai-shujō-shitsu-u-busshō* (一切衆生悉有仏性)

analytic judgment; *bunseki-handan* (分析判断)

antinomical self-identity; see relationship of contradictory self-unity

antinomy; *niritsu-haihan* (二律背反)

a priori synthetic judgment; *sententeki-sōgō-handan* (先天的総合判断)

aspect of mind in thusness (*tathatā*); *shin-shinnyo-mon* (心真如門)

aspect of mind in turbulence (saṃsāra); *shin-shōmetsu-mon*

(心生滅門)

Buddha-nature (field, realm); *busshō* (仏性); *buddhatā,*
  buddhakṣetra

causal conditions; *shuen* (衆縁); *pratyayas*

class consciousness; *kaikyū-ishiki* (階級意識)

clear perception; *kanshō* (観照)

compassion, infinite love; *jihi* (慈悲); *karuṇā*

consciousnes of the mind-base (mind-source); see realization of
  the mind-base

consciousness-only unhampered by external phenomenon;
  yuishiki-mukyō (唯識無境)

continuum; *renzoku-sei* (連続性)

conventional truth; *zokutai* (俗諦); *saṃvṛti-satya*)

cooperation among the specialized fields; *bungyōteki-kyōdō*

(分業的協同)

defilement, obstacled nature of existence; *bonnō* (煩悩);
  kleśa

delusion; see nonenlightenment

determinism; *kettei-ron* (決定論)

diagram of the mind-base (mind-source); *shingen-no-zushiki*

(心源の図式)

dialectic; *benshōhō* (弁証法)

dimension of being; *jigen* (次元)

discriminative knowledge; *funbetsu-chi* (分別智); *vikalpa-buddhi, kalpanā-jñāna*

doctrine, significance; *gi* (義)

element of being, factor of experience; *hō* (法); *dharma*

emptiness, devoid of characteristics; *kū* (空); *śūnyatā*; see also nonbeing

emptiness realized in *prajñā* (wisdom); *hannya-no-kū*
(般若の空)

endless interpenetration of events (realities, elements); *jūjū-mujin* (重重無尽)

enlightenment; *satori* (悟り); *bodhi*, nirvāṇa

enter the pure realm of existence; *ōsō* (往相)

epistemological subjectivism; *ninshikironteki-shukan-shugi*
(認識論的主觀主義)

equality (sameness) qua discrimination (differentiation); *byōdō-soku-sabetsu* (平等即差別)

eschatology; *shūmatsu-shisō* (終末思想)

evil; see unwholesome condition

five aggregates of being; *go-un* (五蘊); *pañca-skandhāḥ*

    corporeality or form; *shiki* (色); *rūpa*

    feeling; *ju* (受); *vedanā*

    imagery; *sō* (想) *saṃjñā*

activity of play of imagery; *gyō* (行); *saṃskāra*

consciousness; *shiki* (識); *vijñāna*

four alternatives; see *tetralemma*

four virtues (characteristics) of nirvāṇa; *shitoku* (四 德)

permanence; *jō* (常)

bliss; *raku* (樂)

true self; *ga* (我)

purity; *jō* (淨)

fundamental diagram; *kihonteki-zushiki* (基本的図式)

good; see wholesome condition

historical materialism; *yuibutsu-shikan* (唯物史觀)

holistic nature of man; *zenjinteki* (全人的)

ignorance, delusory existence; *mumyō* (無明); *avidyā*; see also nonenlightenment

integrative dialectic; *sōgō-benshōhō* (総合弁証法)

intellectual intuition; *chiteki-chokkan* (知的直觀)

interrelational origination, dependent origination; *engi* (緣起), *innen* (因緣); *pratītya-samutpāda*

interrelational origination by (based on) *ālaya-vijñāna* (storehouse consciousness); *araya-shiki-engi* (阿賴耶識緣起)

interrelational origination by (based on) thusness (*tathatā*); *shinnyo-engi* (真如緣起)

intuitive synthetic judgment; *chokkan-teki-sōgō-handan*

（直觀的総合判断）

intuitive unconsciousness; *chokkan-teki-muishiki*

（直觀的無意識）

list of numbered doctrines; *hossū-myōmoku* (法数名目)

logic of alternative; *nisha-takuitsu-no-ronri*

（二者択一の論理）

logic of place; *basho-no-ronri* (場所の論理)

logic of refutation; *hitei-ronri* (否定論理); *prasaṅga*

logic of unity (oneness, undifferentiation); *ichi-no-ronri*

（一の論理）

logicism, discursive reasoning; *ronri-shugi* (論理主義)

mutual entrance and penetration of characteristics (elements);

sōsoku-sōnyū (相即相入)

mutuality of being and nonbeing; *umu-sōsoku* (有無相即)

mutuality of individuality and the whole (totality); *zen-to-ko-ga-sōsoku* (全と個が相即)

mutuality of one and many (all); *itta-sōsoku* (一多相即)

nirvāṇic tranquillity; *nehan-jakujō* (涅槃寂靜)

no separate *dharmic* realm outside the mind; *shinge-mubeppō*

（心外無別法）

nonbeing, voidness, nothingness, *mu* (無); see also emptiness nonenlightenment, delusion; *mayoi* (迷 い); *avidyā, moha*; see also ignorance

nonextinction; *fumetsu* (不滅); *anirodha*

nonorigination; *fushō* (不生); *anutpāda*

one-is-all; *ichi-soku-issai* (一即一切)

One-Mind (singular nature of the mind); *isshin* (一心)

original (primal) vow; *seigan* (誓願); *praṇidhāna*

perception, examination; *kan* (観)

perfect freedom of perception, free unbounded nature of

perception; *kanjizai* (観自在)

philosophy of depth-*prajña* (profound wisdom); *jin-hannya-no-tetsugaku* (深般若の哲学)

principle of holistic nature of man; *zenjinteki-rihō*

(全人的理法)

psychological positivism; *shinri-jisshō-ron*

(心理実証論)

psychological structuralism; *shinri-kōzō-ron*

(心理構造論)

pure experience; *junsui-keiken* (純粋経験)

reality as such; *jissō* (実相)

realization of the mind-base (mind-source); *shingen-no-jikaku*

(心源の自覚)

reason; *risei* (理性)

refutation qua elucidation; *haja-kenshō* (破邪顕正)

relationship of contradictory self-unity (or antinomical self-identity); *mujunteki-jikodōitsu* (矛盾的自己同一); see also self-identity of absolute contradiction

return from the pure realm of existence to help save others; *gensō* (還相)

reversion to ignorance (*avidyā*); *mumyō-tentō* (無明転倒)

rounds of *saṃsāric* (unenlightened) life; *rinne-junkan* (輪廻循環)

rule by law, legalism; *rippō-shugi* (律法主義)

selectivity, chosen (people); *senbetsu-shisō* (選別思想)

self, ego, I; *ga* (我); *ātman, pudgala*

self (personal); *ji* (自)

self-consciousness of absolute nothingness; *zettai-mu-no-jikaku* (絶対無の自覚)

self-embodiment of truth or self-illumination; *jitōmyō* (自燈明)

self-identity of absolute contradiction; *zettai-mujunteki-jiko-dōitsu* (絶対矛盾的自己同一)

sense faculty; *kansei* (感性)

simultaneous penetration; *dōji-sōsoku* (同時相即)

six divine (supernormal) powers; *roku-jinzūriki*

(六神通力); *ṣaḍ-abhijñāḥ*

structure of mind-base (mind-source); *shingen-no-kōzō*

(心源の構造)

sudden rise of discriminative thought that sustains the nature of

ignorance (*avidyā*); *kotsunen-nenki* (忽然念起)

synthetic judgment; *sōgō-handan* (総合判断)

ten profound gates of experiential nature; *jūgen-mon*

(十玄門)

tetralemma (four alternatives, four-cornered logic); *shiku-*

funbetsu (四句分別); *catuṣkoṭi*

three bodies (of the Buddha); sanshin (三身); *trikāya*

body of principle; *hosshin* (法身); *dharmakāya*

body of transformation; *ōjin* (応身); *nirmaṇakāya*

body of bliss; *hōjin* (報身); *sambhogakāya*

Three Greatnesses (of the mind); *sandai* (三大)

greatness of substance; *taidai* (体大)

greatness of form; *sōdai* (相大)

greatness of function; *yūdai* (用大)

three realms of existence; *sangai* (三界); *tri-dhātu*

realm of desire; *yokukai* (欲界); *kāma-dhātu*

realm of form or corporeality; *shikikai* (色界); *rūpa-dhātu*

realm of formless or incorporeality; *mushikikai* (無色界); *arūpya-dhātu*

three realms of existence are reduced to reflection on the singular mind; *sangai-yui-isshin* (三界唯一心)

thusness involving the use of words; *egon-shinnyo* (依言真如)

thusness (*tathatā*) apart from words; *rigon-shinnyo* (離言真如)

thusness of dharma-nature; *shinnyo-hōshō* (真如法性)

thusness of the mind; *shin-shinnyo* (心真如)

total nature of love; *issai-ai* (一切愛); *karuṇā*

total nature of wisdom; *issai-chi* (一切智); *sarvajñata*

transcendental dialectic; *senken-teki-benshō-ron* (先験的弁証論)

truly empty wondrous being; *shinkū-myō-u* (真空妙有)

truth of existence; *hō* (法); *Dharma*

twelvefold interrelational origination; *jūni-engi* (十二縁起); *dvadaśa-pratītya-samutpāda*

Two Aspects (of the mind, i.e., absolute and phenomenal natures); *nimon* (二門)

understanding; *gosei* (悟性)

understanding by means of the whole body (i.e., total being);
tai-ge (体解)

undifferentiation, undifferentiated, nondichotomous; *mibunka*
(未分化)

unitary dialectic; *tanitsu-benshōhō* (単一弁証法)

universal disputation; *fuhen-ronsō* (普遍論争)

unwholesome condition (state); *aku* (悪); *akuśala*

wholesome condition (state); *zen* (善); *kuśala*

wisdom; insight; *chi-e* (智慧); *prajña*

wisdom that fulfills the perceptual process, i.e., transcending the
defiled nature of the senses; *jōsho-satchi* (成所作智)

wisdom that reflects, like a mirror, everything as it is, thereby
transforming into purity the storehouse consciousness (*ālaya-vijñāna*); *daienkyō-chi* (大円鏡智)

wisdom that transcends the defiled nature of the sixth consciousness (*mano-vijñāna*); *myōkan-zatchi*
(妙観察智)

wisdom that transcends the dichotomous nature of discriminative thought (*manas*) to perceive things equally or with
equanimity; *byōdō-shōchi* (平等性智)

Index

Allegory of the Frog in the Well, 40–41; reference to it, 42–52
Ālaya-vijñāna (Storehouse Consciousness), 34–35, 117
Amitayur-dhyāna-sūtra. See *Kanmuryōjukyō*
Anātman, See Non-self
Ātman: grasping phenomenon, 15
Antinomical self-identity. See Relationship of contradictory self-unity
Arithmetic: as related to formal, symbolic and dialectical logic, 92–93
Avalokiteśvara Bodhisattva: first verse of Heart Sūtra, 107–08; dialogue with Śāriputra, 109; as Kanjizai, 109–10
Avataṁsaka ("Garland") Sūtra. See Kegon Sūtra
Avidyā: ignorance or unclear existence, 15, 18, 121–23; non-enlightenment, 34, 37
Awakening of Faith in the Mahāyāna, xiii, 12, 18; concepts of, 21–22; doctrine of One-mind, 51; enlightenment and nonenlightenment, 48; mind-nature, 29; sudden rise of evil, 29; related to Japanese Constitution, 53; true thusness, 12, 33
Axial Age: appearance of philosophic giants, 1–3, 51; names associated with it, 1

Buddha, 1, 3; his words, 4; his teachings, his contributions, 51; his skepticism, 70–71; identity of mind, 9–10, 124; metaphysical questions, 60; teaching of self-reliance, 78
Buddha-nature: endowment of, 15
Buddhism: early thought, 16; Eightfold Noble Path, 76–77; related to methodology in the social sciences, 63–65

Causal nature: two natures, 121
Christianity: contributions of church fathers, 51; holistic consciousness of man, 80
Clear perception (kanshō), 112, 116–17
Cognition: ratio and intellectus, 43; related to TV set receiver, 13; structure of, 13
Comparative philosophy: clarification of thought, 16–17; contrast of ideas, 45–46; future of, 18–19; in fields of epistemology, ontology and metaphysics, 22; methodology of, 17–22, 44–45, 103; need for it, 3–6; related to the diagram of the mind-base, 18–19
Compassion. See Karuṇā
Consciousness, 7–8; bane of limited type, 91–93; holistic nature, 69–72, 93–94; mutual ingression of wisdom and compassion, 79–80; principle of love, 72; related to emptiness, 7–8; related to Three Treasures, 86
Consciousness of the mind-base: diagrams

145